CAVENDISH PRACTICE NOTES

Termination
of
Employment

FOURTH EDITION

JOHN BOWERS QC

LITTLETON CHAMBERS

TEMPLE

LONDON

SERIES EDITOR

CM BRAND, SOLICITOR

Cavendish
Publishing
Limited

London • Sydney

Fourth edition first published in Great Britain 2001 by Cavendish Publishing Limited, The Glass House, Wharton Street, London WC1X 9PX

Telephone: +44 (0)20 7278 8000   Facsimile: +44 (0)20 7278 8080

Email: info@cavendishpublishing.com

Website: www.cavendishpublishing.com

© Bowers, J   2001

Third edition   1995

Fourth edition 2001

Bowers, John, 1956–

Practice notes on termination of employment – 4th ed

1 Employees – dismissal of – Law and legislation – Great Britain

I Title II Termination of employment

344.4'1'012596

ISBN 1 85941 578 4

Printed and bound in Great Britain

Acknowledgments

The author wishes to thank the following colleagues and friends for their assistance on this fourth edition: Julia Palca; Janet Simpson; Ann Goraj; and, in particular, Gary Morton for his assiduous attention to detail. The law is stated as at 5 February 2001.

Contents

1 Basic Information

1.1 Statutes

The Employment Rights Act 1996 (ERA) is the basic consolidating statute of individual employment law. It replaced the Employment Protection (Consolidation) Act 1978, which had itself been amended in various respects by the Employment Acts 1980 and 1982, the Sex Discrimination Act 1986, the Wages Act 1986, the Employment Acts (EA) 1988, 1989, 1990 and 1992 and the Trade Union Reform and Employment Rights Act 1993. The Transfer of Undertakings (Protection of Employment) Regulations 1981 SI 1981/1794, whilst not actually amending the Act, have a major impact on its effects. Some of these are affected by amendments made by the Employment Relations Act 1999. The main sections of ERA relevant to termination of employment are as follows:

1.1.1 Right to return to work after maternity leave

- Section 66 provides the right for a woman to return to work after 29 weeks maternity leave, unless it is not practicable to do so because of redundancy;
- s 69 provides that the employee must give at least 21 days' notice of her return. The employer or employee may postpone that return in certain limited circumstances;
- s 71 provides for not less than 18 weeks ordinary maternity leave with the right to return to work on no less favourable terms and conditions;
- s 73 provides for additional maternity leave if the employee has at the beginning of the 11th week before the expected week of childbirth been continuously employed for not less than one year. She has the right to return to her job within 29 weeks of childbirth;

- r 10 of the 1999 Maternity and Parental Leave Regulations states that if a woman's job is redundant when she is on maternity leave, then the employer must offer her a suitable alternative vacancy if one exists.

1.1.2 Right to minimum period of notice

- Section 86(1) provides that an employee is entitled to one week's notice for each year of continuous service up to a maximum of 12 weeks;
- s 86(2) provides that, where an employee has been employed for more than one month, he must give his employer at least a week's notice.

1.1.3 Right to written statement of reasons for dismissal

- Section 92 provides that an employee with one year's service is entitled to be provided within 14 days of a request with a written statement giving particulars of reasons for dismissal. Irrespective of length of service, if a woman is dismissed when pregnant or on maternity leave, she is entitled to be provided with these reasons (new s 53(1)(2A)).

1.1.4 Unfair dismissal (see 3.2–3.4 below):

- Section 95(1) provides that an employee is dismissed if he is told so with or without notice, his fixed term contract expires without being renewed under the same contract, or he is constructively dismissed;
- s 97(1)–(4) defines the 'effective date of termination';
- ss 96 and 98 state that a failure to permit a woman to return to work after confinement is treated as a dismissal unless the employer and any associated employers did not employ more than five employees and it is not reasonably practicable to permit her to return, or she turns down a reasonable offer of alternative employment, or if it is not reasonably practicable to permit her to return to her job;
- s 98(1) states that the employer has to show the reason, or principal reason, for the dismissal. The reason has to fall within s 57(2) or be some other substantial reason justifying the dismissal of the employee; for
- s 98(2) states that a reason may only be a fair reason for dismissal if it relates to:

- the capability or qualifications of the employee;
- the conduct of the employee;
- redundancy; or
- the contravention by the employer or employee of a duty or restriction imposed by or under any enactment;

- s 98(4)–(6) states that, having found the reason for dismissal, the employment tribunal must determine whether, in the circumstances including the size and administrative resources of the employer's undertaking, the employer acted reasonably in treating it as a sufficient reason for dismissal. This is to be determined in accordance with equity and the substantial merits of the case;

- s 60 provides that a dismissal on the grounds of pregnancy will be unfair unless the employee is incapable of adequately doing the work or to employ her would contravene a statutory duty or restriction;

- s 60A states that dismissal for asserting certain statutory rights shall be unfair;

- s 61 provides that dismissal of an employee taken on to replace a woman on maternity leave is treated as some other substantial reason for dismissal, but the dismissal may still be unfair in all the circumstances;

- s 63 provides that in deciding questions of unfair dismissal, the employment tribunal should disregard any pressure brought to bear on the employer by strikes or other industrial action or threat of such action;

- ss 57A and 99 provide that dismissal on the grounds of pregnancy, childbirth, maternity leave, parental leave or time off to look after dependents will be unfair.

There are special provisions for automatically unfair dismissal with respect to:

(a) health and safety representatives properly carrying out their responsibilities (s 100);

(b) protected shop workers who refuse to work on Sunday (s 101);

(c) workers who refuse to comply with a requirement imposed by the employer in breach of the Working Time Regulations 1998 (s 101A);

(d) occupational pension trustees who carry out their statutory functions (s 102);

(e) employee representatives who carry out their responsibilities in connection with consultation over redundancies or transfers of undertakings (s 103);

(f) employees who make protected disclosures pursuant to the Public Interest Disclosure Act 1998 (s 103A);

(g) employees who have asserted a statutory right (s 104);

(h) employees who have exercised their rights under the National Minimum Wage Act 1998 (s 104A); and

(i) employees who have exercised their rights under the Tax Credits Act 1999 (s 104B).

1.1.5 Remedies for unfair dismissal (see 3.4 below)

* Section 108 provides that an employee cannot bring a claim for unfair dismissal unless he has been employed for more than one year before his dismissal; if he was over the normal retiring age (provided that the normal retiring age is the same for men and women, or if there is no normal retiring age, then the age of 65);

* s 110 states that the Secretary of State may designate dismissal procedure agreements so that employees covered by those procedures must use them and may not claim under the statute. So far, only the scheme between the Electrical Contractors Association and the Amalgamated Engineering and Electricians Union (AEEU) has been so designated;

* s 111 provides that a complaint to an employment tribunal of unfair dismissal must be made within three months from the effective date of termination, or within such further period as the tribunal considers reasonable if it was not reasonably practicable to present within this period;

* ss 115–17 provide that the employment tribunal may make an order for reinstatement or re-engagement. If the complainant is reinstated or re-engaged but the order is not fully complied with, then the tribunal makes an additional award;

* s 118 states that compensation for unfair dismissal may consist of a basic award and compensatory award. An extra compensation award may be made where an order for reinstatement or re-engagement is not complied with;

* s 119 provides for calculation of basic award in a similar manner to a statutory redundancy payment;

* s 123 provides for calculation of compensatory award, including the duty to mitigate; ignoring pressure by a trade union;

contributory fault and set-off of basic award against redundancy payment;

• s 124 sets the limit on the compensatory award, at present £51,700;

• s 75A provides for the calculation of special awards where the reason, or the principal reason, for the dismissal is an inadmissible reason. In calculating this, the tribunal is to take account of compensation already awarded or to be awarded, for sex and/or race and/or disability discrimination or unfair dismissal;

• s 126 allows set-off of compensation for discrimination and unfair dismissal;

• s 128 provides for interim relief in the case of trade union dismissals and under the other provisions:

  ○ s 100(1)(a) and (b) where in a health and safety case a designated employee or workers' representative is dismissed;

  ○ s 102(1) where a trustee of an occupational pension scheme dismissed;

  ○ s 103 where an employee representative is dismissed;

  ○ s 103A where an employee makes a protected disclosure under Public Interest Disclosure Act 1998 (PIDA);

  ○ para 161(2), Sched A1 of the Trade Union and Labour Relations (Consolidation) Act 1992 (TULR(C)A) where an employee is dismissed because he acted with a view to obtaining, preventing, supporting or not supporting union recognition or derecognition under the Central Arbitration Committee's (CAC) statutory recognition procedure.

1.1.6 Redundancy payments

• Section 139 gives the general definition of redundancy, that is the cessation or expected cessation of the business or work in the place where the employee was engaged or the diminution of the requirements for employees to carry out work of a particular kind;

• s 146 sets out the exclusions from redundancy payment: that is, a person over 65; certain terminations by employer on grounds of conduct; the making of a suitable alternative offer of employment which is unreasonably refused;

• s 136 gives a definition of dismissal for redundancy purposes;

• s 141 provides that, if the employee is offered an alternative position, he has in most cases a trial period of four weeks before deciding whether to accept it;

- s 142 states that, if an employee under notice wishes to leave early and the employer objects, the employment tribunal must decide whether it is just and equitable for him to receive the whole or part of the redundancy payment;

- ss 147–50 state that in certain circumstances, an employee placed on lay-off or short time working is entitled to claim a redundancy payment;

- s 153 gives the definition of relevant date for the purposes of a redundancy payment; it is generally the same definition as the effective date of termination.

- s 143 states that, if the employee takes part in a strike or commits misconduct during his period of notice, he is still entitled to a redundancy payment;

- s 139 provides that any act, including death, affecting the employer which terminates the contract of employment is treated as a dismissal for the purposes of a redundancy payment.

1.1.7 Scope of statutory provisions (see 3.1 below)

- Section 191 provides that the Secretary of State for Trade and Industry may make exemption orders in respect of agreed management/trade union redundancy schemes;

- s 159 states that the redundancy payments provisions do not apply to holders of public offices;

- s 164 provides that a claim in respect of a redundancy payment must be made within six months of the relevant date of termination unless the employment tribunal considers it just and equitable to extend time;

- s 165 states that the employer must give the employee written particulars of the calculation of his redundancy pay;

- ss 182–90 state that the employee has certain rights to recover from the National Insurance Fund certain debts due from an insolvent employer, that is, up to eight weeks' arrears of pay; statutory notice pay; up to six weeks' accrued holiday and any unfair dismissal basic award.

1.1.8 Institutions (see Chapters 4–7 below)

- Sections 1–8 of the Employment Tribunals Act 1996 set out the jurisdiction of employment tribunals including the jurisdiction to cover common law employment claims;

* ss 16–17 of the Employment Tribunals Act 1996 makes provisions on recoupment of job seeker's allowance and income support where an employee gains compensation from an employment tribunal: the details are set out in the Employment Protection (Recoupment) Regulations 1996 SI 1996/2349;
* s 18 of the Employment Tribunals Act 1996 sets out the role of Advisory Conciliation and Arbitration Service (ACAS) conciliation officers;
* ss 21–24 of the Employment Tribunals Act 1996 set out the jurisdiction of the Employment Appeal Tribunal (EAT).

1.1.9 Scope of the Act (see 3.1 below)

* Section 191 relate to the application of the Act to Crown employment and House of Commons and House of Lords staff;
* s 197 provides that the employer and employee may agree to exclude the statutory provisions in the case of a contract for a fixed term of one year or more for redundancy purposes only;
* s 199 gives the application of the statute to merchant seamen and share fishermen;
* s 200 gives the application of the statute to police;
* s 203 sets out restrictions on contracting out of the statute;
* s 208 provides that the Secretary of State for Trade and Industry must each year review the limits on the compensation and week's pay in line with the retail price index;
* s 209 gives a general power to amend the Act by order;
* ss 210–17 set out general provisions on continuity of employment;
* s 235 is an interpretation section including the definition of associated employer.

Note also:

(a) Section 152 of TULR(C)A 1992 provides that dismissal for being a member of an independent trade union, taking part in the activities of an independent trade union or refusal to become a member of a trade union is automatically unfair. By ss 237 and 238 of the Act, an employee dismissed during a strike or lock-out may not bring a claim for unfair dismissal unless one or more relevant employees have not been dismissed or a relevant employee has been offered re-engagement within three months of dismissal and the complainant has not been offered re-engagement. There is also a form of 'protected industrial action' under s 238A of TULR(C)A;

• TULR(C)A 1992, s 212A, gives power to ACAS to prepare a scheme for arbitration in unfair dismissal disputes but this has not yet come into force. It is due to commence on 1 April 2001. There is no right of appeal from such arbitrations;

• Race Relations Act 1976 (RRA) outlaws discrimination (including dismissal) on the grounds of race;

• Rehabilitation of Offenders Act 1974 and Rehabilitation of Offenders Act 1974 (Exceptions) Order 1975 (SI No 1023, as amended): unless the position falls into one of the exceptional categories, after the appropriate 'rehabilitation period' an offence is spent and a dismissal on that ground is automatically unfair;

• Sex Discrimination Act 1975, *inter alia,* outlaws dismissals on the ground of sex or marital status;

• ERA 1996, Pt 2, outlaws deductions from wages save in certain circumstances; and

• Human Rights Act 1998: some aspects of the European Convention on Human Rights may be relevant, especially Art 6 on fair trial and Art 8 on respect for private life.

1.2 Statutory instruments

The subject matter of most of the relevant statutory instruments is clear from their titles.

• Employment Tribunals (Constitution and Rules of Procedure) Regulations 1993 SI 1993/2687. For text and commentary, see Bowers, J, Brown, D and Mead, G, *Employment Tribunal Practice and Procedure,* 3rd edn, 1999, Vol 2, pp 210–29.

• Employment Tribunals (Constitution and Rules of Procedure) (Scotland) Regulations 1993 SI 1993/ 2688.

• Industrial Tribunals Awards (Enforcement in Case of Death) Regulations 1976 SI 1976/663.

• Employment Protection (Continuity of Employment) Regulations 1993 SI 1993/660: continuity of employment after reinstatement ordered by employment tribunal.

• Transfer of Undertakings (Protection of Employment) Regulations 1981 SI 1981/1794 (as amended).

• Employment Tribunals (Interest) Order 1990 SI 1990/479) provides for interest to be paid on employment tribunal awards which remain unpaid for 42 days after the Employment Tribunal decision has been sent to the parties (see Bowers, J, Brown, D and Mead, G, *Employment Tribunal Practice and Procedure*, 3rd edn, 1999, Vol 2, pp 206–09).

• Employment Tribunals Extension of Jurisdiction (England and Wales) Order 1994 SI 1994/1623 (see Bowers, J, Brown, D and Mead, G, *Employment Tribunal Practice and Procedure*, 3rd edn, 1999, Vol 2, pp 304–06).

• Employment Tribunals Extension of Jurisdiction (Scotland) Order 1994 SI 1994/1624.

• Employment Appeal Tribunal Rules 1993 SI 1993/2854. This statutory instrument deals with the constitution and administration of the appeal tribunal (the text is set out in Bowers, J, Brown, D and Mead, G, *Employment Tribunal Practice and Procedure*, 3rd edn, 1999, Vol 2, pp 284–302).

• Employment Tribunals (Interest on Awards in Discrimination Cases) Regulations 1996 SI 1996/2803.

1.3 Other sources

The President of the EAT from time to time issues Practice Directions. The most important are on Appeal Procedure of 29 March 1996 and on Preliminary Hearings/Directions given on 10 October 1997.

Codes of Practice: ACAS may issue codes of practice under s 199 of TULR(C)A 1992. There is one of direct relevance to dismissal, on disciplinary practice and procedures in employment (revised 2000); the other two cover the right of recognised trade unions to disclosure of information for collective bargaining purposes and time off for trade union duties and activities. The Secretary of State for Trade and Industry can also issue codes of practice and has done so on industrial action ballots and notices to employers. A breach of a code does not in itself make a person liable, but it may be taken into account just as the Highway Code receives attention in motoring cases. A full list is contained in Chapter 11.

The Commission for Racial Equality also issued a Code of Practice in 1983 and the Equal Opportunities Commission Code of Practice in 1985 and 1997. In addition, a booklet was published in 1990 by HMSO on *Compensation for Loss of Pension Rights for Use in Unfair Dismissal Cases*.

The Code of Practice for the elimination of discrimination in the field of employment against disabled persons or persons who have had a disability was issued in 1996 as was the Guidance on matters to be taken into account in determining questions relating to the definition of 'disability'. Both were issued by the Secretary of State for Education and Employment.

1.4 Case law

A decision in one employment tribunal case is not binding as authority in another tribunal. Although the decisions of the EAT have the force of precedent, the Court of Appeal has, on occasion, deprecated the establishment of fixed principles and guidelines by the EAT. There are well established specialist employment law reports, the Industrial Cases Reports (ICR) and Industrial Relations Law Reports (IRLR). In addition, many unreported cases are collected in *Income Data Services Brief* published by Income Data Services Ltd (IDS) and *Industrial Relations Legal Bulletin*, published by Industrial Relations Services Ltd, both of which appear fortnightly.

1.5 Tribunal and court structures

There is an appeal to the EAT on any question of law arising from a declaration or an order of the CAC, or arising in any proceeding before the CAC (reg 38(8) of the Transnational Information and Consultation of Employees Regulations 1999 SI 1999/3323).

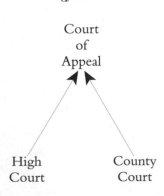

Wrongful dismissal

Court
of
Appeal

High   County
Court   Court

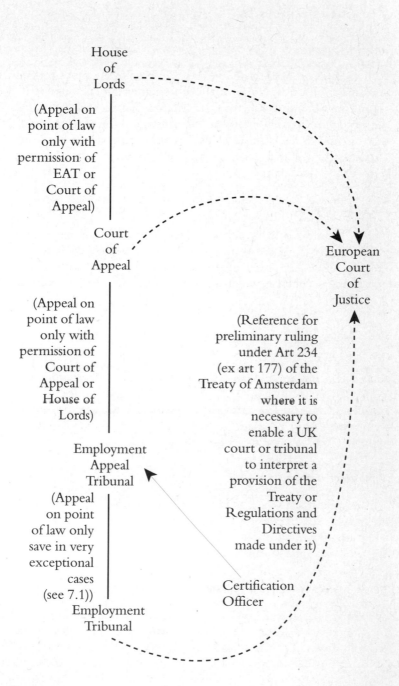

House
of
Lords

(Appeal on
point of law
only with
permission of
EAT or
Court of
Appeal)

Court
of
Appeal

(Appeal on
point of law
only with
permission of
Court of
Appeal or
House of
Lords)

Employment
Appeal
Tribunal

(Appeal
on point
of law only
save in very
exceptional
cases
(see 7.1))

Employment
Tribunal

European
Court
of
Justice

(Reference for
preliminary ruling
under Art 234
(ex art 177) of the
Treaty of Amsterdam
where it is
necessary to
enable a UK
court or tribunal
to interpret a
provision of the
Treaty or
Regulations and
Directives
made under it)

Certification
Officer

1.6 Basic concepts

Unfair dismissal

A dismissal is deemed to be unfair if the employer cannot prove that it was carried out for one of the potentially fair reasons, or if the reason was potentially fair, and the tribunal decides that the employer did not act reasonably in all the circumstances (on this latter aspect, there is no burden of proof). The application must be made to an employment tribunal within three months of the effective date of termination (see Chapter 3).

Wrongful dismissal

This is a dismissal in breach of contract and a claim can be made within six years of the dismissal to the county court or the High Court, or within three months of the date of dismissal in the employment tribunal, which may award only up to a maximum of £26,700.

Redundancy

This concerns a dismissal on the grounds that the employer no longer requires an employee in the place where the employee was employed or to do work of the particular kind carried on by the employee. In the case of a dispute on redundancy payment, an application must be made to an employment tribunal within six months of the relevant date of termination.

Trade union dismissal

This is a dismissal which is by reason of membership or activities of an independent trade union or because of a closed shop. In this event, the potential amount of compensation is much greater than in the ordinary unfair dismissal case (see 3.5.3).

Public Interest Disclosure Dismissal

A dismissal because an employee has made a public interest disclosure as defined in the ERA 1996 is automatically unfair and there is no maximum award. There is also a possibility of claiming interim relief. It is not possible to agree in a compromise agreement or elsewhere that an employee will not in future make a public interest disclosure.

In addition to unfair dismissal and redundancy claims, which are the main focus of this book, the employment tribunals also have jurisdiction over equal pay, discrimination, consultation and redundancies, explusion from a trade union and deductions from wages, as well as several other specialist jurisdictions which give rise to little work. For full list, see Bowers, J, Brown, D and Mead, G, *Employment Tribunal Practice and Procedure*, 3rd edn, 1999.

2 First Questions

2.1 First interview with the employee

Be clear about the client's objective in bringing the claim, that is, whether it is to be reinstated, compensated, to clear his name, or to seek revenge (although this is not a good motive, and one which may lead to an order for costs being made against him). Make it clear that you can only advise on what is available to the client through the courts and employment tribunals and that you have to give advice objectively and dispassionately. Consider whether the employee can gain advice and/or representation through a trade union, Citizens Advice Bureau, Law Centre, the Free Representation Unit, the Bar *Pro Bono* Unit, etc.

Establish the employee's employment history/profile including details of the following:

(a) The size of the employer's undertaking; whether there is a separate personnel department: these matters may be important in assessing the fairness of the dismissal since the employment tribunal has to take account of the 'size and administrative resources of the employer's undertaking' (see 3.2 below).

(b) Any associated employer; often the employee will be vague about who his own employer is, let alone the other companies in a group; it may be necessary to do a company search, and useful to draw up a company structure chart in complex cases.

(c) The employee's record, that is details of any disciplinary 'offences' and sickness and other absences; check whether warnings are still 'active' or have run their course.

(d) The date of commencement (what is the length of continuous employment?) and the effective date of termination of employment. Check whether there has been at any stage of the employment a transfer of an undertaking from one employer to another.

(e) What was the precise work done by the employee and what additional or varied work he could by his contract be required to do?

(f) What was the place where the employment was to be carried out? Could the employer vary that place of employment at will?

(g) The level of pay, split into basic, overtime, bonus pay, unsocial hours premium, etc; query the nature of any bonus: are they *ex gratia*, regular, dependent on productivity/profitability/key tasks, etc?

(h) 'Fringe benefits', such as:

- payment of telephone bills;
- BUPA subscription, permanent health or accident insurance;
- luncheon vouchers or subsidised canteen facilities;
- free or reduced rate accommodation;
- discounts for goods sold, supplied or manufactured by the employer;
- membership of clubs, professional associations, learned societies or health clubs;
- provision of a car or car allowance; did he receive free petrol for business and/or private mileage?
- share options: when could they be exercised? Would the employee have had the means and desire to exercise the options? What is the subscription price? What is the current market price? What is the provision for exercise on termination?
- pension: is it a contributory or non-contributory scheme; is it administered by the employer or a third party; to what extent is it 'portable' to other employment or self-employment? Check if it is a contributory scheme and whether contracted in or out of SERPS.
- was there any profit-related pay scheme?
- check the tax treatment of these benefits, with the twin aims of ensuring that the contract is not tainted with illegality and assessing the likely award of compensation since the compensatory award covers only the net amount of loss of pay and benefits.

(i)   The contract of employment – Are there written agreements, statements of terms of employment, works notices, letters, etc? What are the relevant customs and practices (if any)? Is there a relevant collective bargain, and if so is it clearly incorporated into the individual contract of employment and is the contract automatically varied when the collective agreement is renegotiated?

(j)   The extent of trade unionism in the employer's undertaking and where there is a works council or staff committee.

(k)   Any benefit received since the dismissal.

(l)   The normal hours worked and the basis on which any extra hours were worked, for example, by agreement, at management's discretion.

(m)   The taking of holidays and holiday pay

(n)   How was the contract of employment terminated?

(o)   What was the normal retirement age?

(p)   What is the applicant's date of birth? He may be above normal retiring age and, in any event, the age will be relevant to the calculation of the basic award.

(q)   What procedures apply in the workplace (if any)?

(r)   Was there a workforce agreement, for example, in respect of maternity and parental leave?

Gather together all the relevant documents: this 'trawl' will often be disappointingly small; consider what documents should be in the possession of the employer which the employee will need to establish his case. These relevant documents are likely to include the contract of employment, relevant collective agreements, letters or other documents, varying the contract, regarding the employer's financial condition, or the employee's conduct.

Ask whether the employee has exhausted any internal appeals procedure. This is important because the employment tribunal will probably expect the employee to have done so; the procedure may also make clearer the reasons for dismissal and show weaknesses in the management's case (especially if witnesses are called); and the matter may be resolved without the need for recourse to an employment tribunal. The tribunal may reduce any award by up to two weeks' pay if internal procedures have not been adopted (s 127A of the Employment Relations Act 1996 (ERA)).

Consider whether the employer has given full written reasons for the dismissal; if not, make a request by letter for those reasons. The employer has 14 days from receiving the request in which to respond. But don't expect a fully pleaded case from the employer at this stage; the statute does not require that to be done. If the claim involves sex, disability or race discrimination, consider whether to apply for answers to the special questionnaire which is available from the Commission for Racial Equality, Disability Rights Commission and Equal Opportunities Commission (see Bowers, J, Brown, D and Mead, G, *Employment Tribunal Practice and Procedure*, 1999, p46).

If the reason for dismissal is clearly stated by the employer, consider whether it is the true reason for dismissal or whether the employer in fact acted out of a different motivation, for example, because of the employee's trade union activities, because the employer needed to cut costs, because the employee blew the whistle on the employer, or by reason of a personality clash;

Does the client retain any company property or documents? Customer lists are especially sensitive and the employer may seek a search order if he thinks that the employee may have retained confidential information at his premises (see Bean, D, *Injunctions*, 6th edn, 1994 for full discussion). In most cases, the employer has the right to recover a company car when an employee is dismissed.

Has the client gained other work: what are the prospects of his doing so? It is vital that the client is realistic (and honest) about alternative jobs. Many employees do not appreciate the importance of mitigation. Where the dismissal leaves the employee bitter, he may seek to ensure that the 'bill' for the employer is a big one. A shop floor worker cannot hold himself available only to take work as manager of Grimsby Town Football Club! He must take reasonable steps to gain other employment or self employed work. He should keep a full list of all jobs applied for and the response, together with a list of the sources of such jobs (for example, local newspaper, 'word of mouth', professional journal, Job Centre).

What form of representation (if any) is appropriate to the case? In some cases, a party may easily represent himself, whilst others are highly complex and will benefit from having representation by an experienced solicitor or barrister because they, for example, require skillful cross-examination, or involve difficult points of law.

The employee/potential applicant may well be eligible for assistance through the Legal Services Commission. This means you have to establish your priorities very quickly and decide how best you can assist the applicant. A trade union, Citizens Advice Bureau, the Free Representation Unit, a Law Centre or another *pro bono* unit may also be able to provide assistance. The employee may have legal expenses insurance which covers the claim.

Assess whether the employee will make a good witness and what other witnesses are available or may be made to attend by a witness order.

Ensure that the client realises at the outset:

(a) the possible prejudicial effect on future employment should potential employers discover that he has taken a case to an employment tribunal, especially if he loses (and do not underestimate in any case the local or industry 'grapevine' although the likelihood of a case being referred to in the press varies considerably from area to area);

(b) the anxiety and stress which an employment tribunal may cause to the employee and his witnesses;

(c) the cost of proceeding to a hearing and the fact that he is unlikely to recover costs from the employer even if he wins the case (see 6.4 below);

(d) the inability of the employment tribunal to order the employer to provide the employee with a reference, and an unsuccessful application to an employment tribunal may be the worst sort of 'anti/negative reference' to a potential employer; the provision of a reference may, however, be an important provision in the overall settlement of the claim;

(e) that the likelihood of reinstatement or re-engagement is remote (see 3.5.1 below);

(f) that the press may report the tribunal and may sensationalise the evidence given (the risk of extensive publicity is perhaps greater in a small town than in a city); but in sex and disability discrimination cases, a restricted reporting order may be available to restrain press coverage until the decision has been given;

(g) that if he loses before the employment tribunal, an appeal will not succeed, unless there is a true point of law involved (see 7.1 below);

(h) that the employer may have a 'deeper purse' than the employee and may treat the defence to the claim as 'a matter of principle' since the result may have an impact on general practices in the workplace, on his relationship with the trade union and/or disciplinary measures in the case of all other employees (perhaps other cases are 'in the pipeline');

(i) the likely need to have supporting witnesses: if they still work for the same employer/respondent, they may be reluctant to come forward and it is never a good idea to rely on unwilling witnesses who attend only because compelled to do so (see 5.4.5 below);

(j) the fact that it may be several months before a hearing is held, some weeks thereafter for the decision to be promulgated and an appeal may be launched after that which may take over a year to be heard;

(k) the fact that success in the employment tribunal will have no direct effect on criminal proceedings and *vice versa*;

(l) that the short time limits for bringing claims will not be extended merely because negotiations are continuing with an employer;

(m) that if an employee is ordered to be reinstated or re-engaged by an employment tribunal (which only happens in a small minority of cases), there is no power to enforce such an order: the employer will merely have to pay extra compensation if he refuses to comply with such an order.

Tactical decisions: is it sensible to bring a claim for wrongful dismissal as well as unfair dismissal? In most cases, the employer will either have given the employee payment in lieu of notice or the notice claim will be too small to justify proceedings, since the length of notice required will be short and contained within the compensation likely to be awarded for unfair dismissal. Consider the possibility of bringing other related claims, for example, failure to provide written reasons for dismissal, an unlawful deduction under the Pt II of the ERA 1996, wrongful dismissal and failure to provide itemised pay statement or a stress claim. The most important considerations are that:

(a) it will be appropriate to bring a separate wrongful dismissal claim when the employee is in a high status occupation with a long period of notice by express agreement or by reason of an implied term of reasonable notice (perhaps two years in the case of a senior company director). Indeed his likely compensation may be well above the statutory limits for unfair dismissal; it is possible to make a claim in the employment tribunal but it can award only up to £25,000; there is no maximum limit for a claim in the civil courts;

(b) a dismissal may be wrongful yet the employer behaved reasonably in all the circumstances so that the dismissal is not unfair, or *vice versa*;

(c) the employer may seek an adjournment of the tribunal case pending a determination by the High Court if the claim is over £25,000 and thus cannot be brought to recover the full amount in the employment tribunal (see 5.5.4 below);

(d) certain heads of loss are treated differently in the employment tribunal and High Court and in particular the methods of calculating pension loss are more favourable to the employee in unfair dismissal claims; the length of time over which loss of earnings are awarded will probably be greater in unfair dismissal than wrongful dismissal proceedings, since in wrongful dismissal proceedings the court will not make an award of damages over a period longer than the notice period;

(e) legal aid is available for wrongful dismissal cases in the county court or High Court, but not for any claim brought in the employment tribunal (except in Scotland);

(f) costs are normally recoverable from the unsuccessful other party in civil cases but very rarely so in employment tribunal cases; by the same token, the employee will have to pay the other party's costs, if he loses in wrongful dismissal in the county or High Court but not unfair dismissal claims.

Is this a case which may settle? If settlement is a possibility or a desirability, develop a strategy for dealing with the ACAS Conciliation Officer or directly with the other side in order to achieve a compromise. Should he float a figure? Or would a round table discussion be more helpful? Will time heal any outstanding bitterness by the employer? Is a 'door of the tribunal' settlement the only realistic option? Check whether the employee has already obtained any payment and whether there has been any 'informal' negotiations about settlement. Also, check whether he has obtained another job and if so what is the wage or salary.

Is this a case where the employee may gain an injunction to prevent the dismissal? (see Bowers, J, *Bowers on Employment Law*, 5th edn, 2000).

You should now be in a position to advise your client, and you should cover at least the following issues:

(a) advise the client, on the information you have received, whether or not he has an arguable claim for unfair dismissal;

(b) advise him as to the likely financial benefit if he wins the case in the employment tribunal and the costs of taking the case (this will, of course, include consideration of what form of representation is necessary) and the various options as to this;

(c) consider whether a wrongful dismissal or an unfair dismissal claim or both are appropriate;

(d) inform the client of the possible non-legal considerations in taking an employment tribunal claim and the possible benefits – adverse publicity for the employer, money, feelings of vindication: the satisfaction of having the 'day in court';

(e) discuss possibilities of settlement and realistic terms on which the case might be settled. Suggest that a letter before action be written and 'without prejudice' negotiations started before commencing proceedings and stress that settlement is always preferable to an employment tribunal case, particularly because of the risks and costs involved;

(f) note that the employment tribunal has no power to grant a reference;

(g) advise the client that for unfair dismissal or discrimination claims an originating application, IT1, must be lodged with the central or relevant Regional Office of Employment Tribunals (ROET) within three months of the effective date of termination.

Is there any possibility of a work related stress claim?

2.2   Originating application: Form IT1

A standard Originating Application Form IT1 (Chapter 9) is adopted for all employment tribunal claims. Some of the questions are not, however, appropriate to particular claims, and the relevance of others is not clear at first sight. I consider here those which cause the most trouble.

Question 1 – Question for the tribunal to decide: you should clearly identify (all) the applicant's cause(s) of action. It is perfectly proper (and often desirable) to combine claims, for example, for unfair dismissal and/or redundancy payment and/or sex discrimination. The response to the question in an unfair dismissal claim would typically be 'whether I have been unfairly dismissed' and in a redundancy case 'whether I have a right to a redundancy payment and the amount of redundancy payment to which I am entitled'.

Question 2 – Date of birth: this may be relevant to decide potential exclusion from the right to claim, the amount of a redundancy payment and the level of basic award.

Question 3 – Place of work: this may be important in deciding the right to a redundancy payment, or whether an employee has disobeyed a reasonable instruction in refusing to move to another place of work.

Question 5 – Applicant's occupation or position: only a brief answer is normally called for. In cases of dispute or where the matter has a particular relevance (such as redundancy), a further elaboration should be given in the answer to question 12.

Question 8 – Date of commencement and termination of employment: these are important in determining whether the employee has the qualifying period to claim and the amount of any redundancy payment or basic award to be made. Ensure that the effective date of termination is stated as it is defined by statute (see 3.2.2 below).

Question 10 – Details of complaint: applicants often find that there is not enough space under this question to have their full say. By all means add further pages and exhibit relevant correspondence, if this is appropriate. Remember that this is the first document an employment tribunal will see regarding the case and it is important that it makes a good first impression. Scrappy, ill-thought-out and barely legible screeds are too common and should be avoided. Be careful not to commit the employee in the Originating Application to statements which he will not be able to prove at a hearing.

Question 11 – Remedies: although the form asks what remedy the applicant seeks, he is not irretrievably bound by the answer. He may, for example, enter 'compensation' and at a later stage decide that he does wish to be reinstated or re-engaged. Indeed, when an applicant is successful, the employment tribunal must ask what remedy he seeks. Only then is he put to a formal 'election'. It is sometimes tactically wise to claim reinstatement, even though this is not really seriously sought, in the hope of gaining a better settlement. It will often be appropriate to refer to an attached sheet: if so, the sheet should set up clear propositions in numbered paragraphs. The *Understanding ITs* booklet published by the Employment Tribunals Service has a list of post codes against the name of the regional office of the ET to which the IT1 is to be sent.

2.3   First interview with employer (respondent to an employment tribunal claim)

Carefully consider the Originating Application: is it desirable to seek Further and Better Particulars or to ask a detailed set of questions? Are the details as to dates, payment and hours of work correct?

Are there any jurisdictional barriers which may defeat the claim? If so, write to the (ROET) seeking a preliminary hearing to rule on these points (see 5.4 below).

Assess the strengths and weaknesses of the employer's case. Did the employee deserve to be dismissed? Was the procedure adopted fair? Are the available documents consistent with the employer's case? Does the employee have sufficient evidence so that even if the procedure adopted was unfair, little or no compensation will be awarded because it was fair in substance.

Review all the documents: in most cases, the employer will have much more paperwork in his possession than the employee. Consider carefully past disciplinary warnings (are they 'spent'?), notes of hearings and appeals (it may save a great deal of time at the employment tribunal itself if such notes can be agreed beforehand or at least that the applicant openly states what aspects he will challenge). If the case proceeds to a hearing, typed transcripts should be made available.

Is the applicant's case so weak that it is worth asking for a pre-hearing review? Unless the case is wholly unsustainable, a pre-hearing review may be more trouble than it is worth because:

(a) it requires two attendances at the employment tribunal by the representative if not the witnesses;

(b) even if a deposit is ordered, the applicant may still pursue the case;

(c) if a deposit is not ordered, it may boost the applicant's morale, and the employment tribunal may in the course of the hearing suggest to the employee ways in which he may put his case better, or documents which may help him to make his case (see 5.4 below).

Is the applicant likely to gain alternative employment or engage in self employment? Assess potential jobs open to the applicant in the locality and beyond. Unfortunately for the employer, it is usually impossible to gain an order from the employment tribunal for particulars of the steps taken by the employee to mitigate his loss before liability is determined.

Should you write a 'Calderbank letter', that is, an offer without prejudice save as to costs? There is no 'payment in' procedure in employment tribunals and employment tribunals are generally reluctant to award costs (see 6.4 below). It is, however, possible to write a 'Calderbank letter' making an offer to settle the case 'without prejudice' but reserving the right to show it to the tribunal after the hearing when costs are to be considered. This will not, however, always lead to a costs order in favour of the writer of the letter even if the applicant secures less from a tribunal award than was on offer in the letter. You may wish to offer the applicant his old job back or an alternative position.

Consider which witnesses will be available and necessary to support the case; are they likely to be unable or reluctant to attend the hearing?

Check the jobseeker's allowance questionnaire: if the applicant has applied for allowance and has been initially disqualified, the employer may be sent a questionnaire. This will ask whether the employer dismissed the employee and if so the reason. It is important to ensure that the contents of the Forms IT3 and UB86 tell the same story.

Ensure that the employer realises:

(a) that he is very unlikely to be able to recover costs from an unsuccessful applicant and what the likely costs are;

(b) that a decision by one tribunal on the facts of a case is not authority in a later case, so that even if he wins one case, it will not be decisive in other (even similar) circumstances, although it may discourage others from 'having a go';

(c) the time involved in defending the proceedings; many employers complain more about the management time which has to be spent on preparing for and attending an employment tribunal case than about the legal costs themselves;

(d) that, if the employer settles cases too easily, it may gain a reputation as a 'soft touch';

(e) the possibility of bad publicity and the effect on relations with other employees. (For questions to be asked under each heading of dismissal, see 3.3 below.)

2.4   Notice of appearance

The following numbers indicate the paragraphs on the standard Notice of Appearance form (see Chapter 9):

Para 1 – Name of the respondent: the applicant may have incorrectly stated the respondent's name. There is no point in seeking to avoid liability on this basis since the employment tribunal will readily give leave to the applicant to amend the name given, even at the hearing.

Para 3 – Whether the claim is to be resisted: the employer may admit the claim altogether or admit that he is liable for a redundancy payment but not unfair dismissal which is also claimed, or for some part of the claim.

Para 8 – Grounds of defence: it is possible to 'plead in the alternative', in other words, to state that the applicant is not entitled to bring the claim because he worked abroad, but if this is found by the employment tribunal to be incorrect, then the applicant was fairly dismissed. An employer may also state the reason as being, for example, misconduct or in the alternative incapability where the facts straddle the thin dividing line between the two concepts. Similarly, there may be a genuine legal issue/dispute as to whether a given set of circumstances constitutes dismissal on the grounds of redundancy or some other substantial reason for dismissal, namely reorganisation. It is, however, vital that the employer is clear as to the factual reason for his dismissal (and that this is consistent with the reason already given in the letter of dismissal and/or internal hearing and/or internal appeal), whatever is the statutory label in s 98 of the ERA 1996 to be attached to those facts.

Remember that the tribunal members may see this form well in advance of the hearing, and it will in any case be the first indication of the employer's case. Do not treat it like a High Court 'pleading' but do state the full facts clearly and fully. Tribunals are not impressed by a generalised 'plea' which leaves more questions than answers, and cries out for a Request for Further and Better Particulars to be made or causes them to doubt that the employer knows why he dismissed the employee.

It is relatively easy to gain from the employment tribunal an extension of the 21 day period to enter an appearance, and a response presented out of time is deemed to include an application for extension of time. To be safe, you should give reasons in your application why an extension is required.

Check very carefully whether the period of service and the level of pay claimed by the applicant is accurate. This information may have an important effect on jurisdiction and level of award.

2.5 Procedural checklist

This list sets out the typical sequence of procedures in an unfair dismissal case. Tribunals are being encouraged to 'case manage' applications in the manner of the civil courts since the Woolf reforms. The extent to which this occurs differs between different regions, but some will, for example, list all discrimination cases for at least one directions hearing, so that the issues can be properly set out and the scope of the hearing clearly identified.

*   An Originating Application is presented to the relevant Office of Employment Tribunal; Employment Tribunal Rules, r 1(1) (see 4.2).
*   The Secretary of Tribunals may refuse to register the Originating Application on grounds that the employment tribunal has no jurisdiction or that the claim is out of time. If he refuses, the application will not proceed unless the applicant informs the Secretary to the Tribunal that he wishes to do so; Employment Tribunal Rules, r 1(2)(3). If the Application is registered:
*   the respondent must serve a Notice of Appearance within 21 days of receipt of the Originating Application; Employment Tribunal Rules, rr 2 and 3. The employment tribunal may extend this timescale. (Note that the following steps may take place in any order.)
*   The respondent may seek to strike out the Originating Application; rr 13(2)(d), (e) and (f) of the Employment Tribunal Rules. First write to the ROET clearly setting out your reasons why the case should be struck out. The ROET will send this letter to the other parties in the case asking for comments, and confirm the chairman's decision by letter. If you are dissatisfied with the decision and consider that there is a prospect of overturning or altering it, ask for an interlocutory hearing to be held; if not:
*   either party may seek leave to amend their 'pleadings'. Leave will almost certainly be granted in a letter and a copy of the amended Originating Application or Notice of Appearance is then circulated to the other party or parties.

- Either party or the tribunal of its own motion may seek Further and Better Particulars of the other's pleadings or propose questions designed to draw out the issues in the case and see the scope of the dispute between the parties; Employment Tribunal Rules, r 4(1)(a). First write to your opponent(s) asking for the particulars and giving him/them, say, seven days to reply; if he does not reply to your satisfaction, write to the ROET clearly setting out your case why the particulars are necessary. The ROET will send this letter to the other parties in the case asking for comments and probably give a decision by letter. If you are dissatisfied with the decision and consider that there is a prospect of overturning it, ask for an interlocutory hearing to be held.

- Each party may request discovery and inspection of documents in the possession of the other; Employment Tribunal Rules, r 4(1)(b). First write to your opponent asking for discovery of particular documents or groups of documents and giving him, say, seven days to reply. If he does not reply to your satisfaction, write to the ROET clearly setting out your case why the documents are necessary to your case. The ROET will send this letter to the other parties in the case asking for comments, and probably give a decision by letter. If you are dissatisfied with the decision and consider that there is a prospect of overturning it, ask for an interlocutory hearing to be held.

- Either party may apply for witness orders and that the witness produce any relevant document; Employment Tribunal Rules, r 4(2). Write to the ROET clearly setting out in general terms what evidence may be given by the witness, the extent to which the evidence is relevant to the issues in the case, and why the witness is unwilling or unable to attend voluntarily. The ROET will probably give a decision on this point by letter. If you are dissatisfied with the decision and consider that there is a prospect of overturning it (and there usually will not be), ask for an interlocutory hearing to be held. The witness may himself apply to set aside the order, but this will be permitted only in rare circumstances if his evidence is likely to be relevant. It is very unlikely that you will gain a witness order in respect of a hostile witness.

- A party may apply for or the tribunal may order a pre-hearing review at which the tribunal will have to decide whether the application or (in rare cases) the response has a reasonable prospect of success. If not, the tribunal may order a deposit of up to £500 (recently increased from £150) to be lodged as a condition of the claim proceeding; Employment Tribunal Rules, r 6. Write to the ROET clearly setting out why you consider a pre-hearing review is desirable.

- The tribunal (of its own motion or on the application of a party) may order a preliminary hearing to determine whether it has jurisdiction to hear a claim (for example, because the claim has not been presented in time). First write to your opponent stating clearly why you consider that a preliminary hearing would be desirable and conducive to saving time and costs, and asking whether he would join you in making a joint application to the employment tribunal to achieve this end. After receiving the reply, write (or make a joint application) to the ROET clearly setting out your case why a preliminary hearing is likely to save time and costs and defining the issues clearly. The ROET will send this letter to the other parties in the case asking for their comments, and probably give a decision by letter. If you are dissatisfied with the decision and consider that there is a prospect of overturning it, ask for an interlocutory hearing to be held.

- If the case has settled, the employment tribunal may at any time dismiss the application upon its withdrawal; Employment Tribunal Rules, r 13(2)(a) and/or make a consent order; Employment Tribunal Rules, r 13(2)(b).

- The tribunal may adjourn the hearing date: Employment Tribunal Rules, r 13(7). First write to your opponent stating clearly why you consider that the hearing date should be vacated (for example, because witnesses are unavailable; because the case will last longer than the allotted time; because other proceedings are pending etc) and asking whether he would join you in making a joint application to the employment tribunal to achieve this end. After receiving the reply, write (or make a joint application) to the ROET clearly setting out your case why the tribunal hearing date should be postponed. The ROET will send this letter to the other parties in the case asking for comments, and probably notify them of the chairman's decision by letter. If you are dissatisfied with the decision and consider that there is a prospect of overturning it, ask for an interlocutory hearing to be held.

- Either party may apply to have a party joined to the proceedings. Write to the ROET stating why it is necessary to effect the joinder. The ROET will probably give a decision by letter. Employment Tribunal Rules, r 17(1). The employment tribunal may also order one party to defend a claim on behalf of all persons having the same interest; Employment Tribunal Rules, r 17(3).

- Either party may apply to have the case considered together with others, or the employment tribunal may order this to be done of its own motion; Employment Tribunal Rules, r 18.

- Either party may request that the whole hearing or a part of the hearing may be heard in private; Employment Tribunal Rules, r 8(1). First write to the other party asking whether it is prepared to agree to such a request. When a reply is received, write to the ROET setting out the reasons why you consider that the hearing or a part should be held in private. The ROET will probably give a decision in writing. If you are dissatisfied with the decision and think that there is a prospect of overturning it, ask for an interlocutory hearing to be held. A company will not, however, be successful in an application merely on the grounds of the adverse publicity which it fears may arise from a hearing. Such cases are rare, save in cases including children and national security considerations. In cases of sexual misconduct or some disability discrimination cases, an application may be made for a restricted reporting order (ss 11 and 12 of the Employment Tribunals Act 1996 (ETA)).

- Either party may submit written representations to the employment tribunal but this must be done at least seven days before the hearing and served on the other side; Employment Tribunal Rules, r 8(1). You should only take this course in cases of dire necessity, since oral evidence will be much more effective.

- The ROET must give notice of hearing at least 14 days before the hearing is due to take place, or may give less time with the consent of the parties (Employment Tribunal Rules, r 5(2)). Usually, longer periods of notice of the hearing are given in fact.

- The hearing is held: for details see below, 6.1–6.2.

- The decision is given either orally at the hearing with the written reasons to follow, or as a reserved written decision; Employment Tribunal Rules, r 10.

- If the decision is initially given in summary form, either party may request reasons in an extended form at the hearing or within 21 days after the summary decision was sent to the parties; Employment Tribunal Rules, r 10(4).

- Either party may apply for costs. This application should be made either at the hearing or within a reasonable time after the hearing initially by letter; Employment Tribunal Rules, r 12.

- Either party may apply for a review of the decision at the hearing or within 14 days of the written decision being sent to the parties; Employment Tribunal Rules, r 11(1)–(4). Such an application may, however, be rejected by the tribunal chairman if he considers that it has no reasonable prospect of success. If it is not dealt with in this summary manner, the whole tribunal reviews the decision, and may confirm, vary or revoke it. If the decision is revoked, the case will, if necessary, be reheard before the same or a differently constituted tribunal; Employment Tribunal Rules, r 11(5)–(7).

- If there is no appeal, and the respondent has failed to pay the compensation or costs awarded, or the applicant has failed to meet a costs order, the appropriate party in whose favour the award has been made should apply to the county court to enforce the order.

- Interest is usually calculated from 42 days after the original decision was sent to the parties but there is special provision in discrimination cases; Employment Tribunals (Interest on Awards in Discrimination Cases) Regulations 1996 SI 1996/2803.

- In the case of an appeal, the appellant completes a Notice of Appeal in the form set out in the Employment Appeal Tribunal (EAT) Rules 1993 SI 1993/2854 (see Chapter 9) and sends it to the appropriate address for England and Wales or Scotland within 42 days from the date on which full written reasons for the decision of the employment tribunal were sent to the appellant. If the Notice of Appeal is sent to the EAT out of time, an application may be made to the EAT registrar to extend time for appeal, although such applications are rarely granted. An application may be made by letter, setting out all the reasons for the delay. The registrar will send a copy to the other party/parties to the appeal asking for comments. The registrar will give a decision in writing. If you are dissatisfied with that decision, and consider that there is a prospect of overturning it, you may apply for an oral hearing; EAT Rules, r 3(1)(2). If summary reasons are given for the decision, apply to the employment tribunal for reasons in an extended form within 21 days of receiving the summary reasons.

- Where it appears to the registrar that the grounds of appeal do not give the EAT grounds to entertain jurisdiction, the registrar will inform the appellant, and no further action will be taken on the appeal unless:

(a) the appellant serves a fresh notice of appeal; or

(b) the appellant expresses his dissatisfaction with the decision, in which case the matter will be considered by a judge; EAT Rules, r 13(3)–(6).

- The EAT sends the Notice of Appeal to the respondent(s); EAT Rules, rr 4 and 5.

- The respondent may submit a respondent's notice similar to Form 4 attached to the EAT Rules (see Chapter 9). He may cross-appeal from the whole or any part of the decision (although not merely on the basis that the reasons for the decision were incorrect). If he does not wish to resist the appeal, the EAT may make an agreed order upholding the appeal, or indeed on any terms agreed between the parties (this may usually be done by letter); EAT Rules, r 6.

- Most appeals are set down for a preliminary hearing when the EAT will decide whether there is any prospect of success in the absence of the respondent. If it does not consider that there is any such prospect, it may strike out the appeal; EAT Practice Direction (there is a transitional pilot scheme in place at the time of writing).

- The EAT may of its own motion or on the application of any party, direct that a party be joined to or dismissed from the proceedings; EAT Rules, r 18.

- The EAT may of its own motion or on application by a party, hold an appointment for directions. All interlocutory applications, at any other time, should be made to the EAT Registrar, and there is an appeal to a judge. An appointment will usually only be held in complex cases with several parties, or when different issues need to be determined in advance of the hearing of the appeal itself; EAT Rules, rr 19–25.

- If a party fails to deliver a respondent's notice, the EAT may order that he be debarred from taking any further part in the proceedings, or make any other order it thinks fit; EAT Rules, r 26.

- The EAT may, of its own motion or on the application of a party within 14 days from the date of the order, review its decision; EAT Rules, r 33.

- A party may apply for costs either at the hearing of the appeal or shortly thereafter; EAT Rules, r 34. An appeal from the EAT does not suspend enforcement of its order subject to any directions on such appeal or by the EAT itself; EAT Rules, r 31(3).

- In a case where the appeal appears to involve allegations of commission of a sexual offence or evidence of a personal nature in a disability case, the registrar is to omit any identifying feature and the EAT may make a restricted reporting order; EAT Rules, rr 23 and 23A.

- Further appeal might be made to the Court of Appeal with permission of the EAT or Court of Appeal itself.

3 Unfair Dismissal

3.1 Considerations

3.1.1 Is the employee qualified to bring a claim?

(a) Is the person an employee or engaged under a contract for service?: this is a question of fact in each case, but tribunals pay particular attention to the degree of control exercised over the worker, the degree of integration into the enterprise and whether the worker brings his own equipment. The description which the parties give to their relationship is not decisive since it may be intended to avoid or minimise taxation obligations.

(b) Some employment legislation, in particular unfair dismissal and redundancy payments apply only to employees, but both employees and others who personally execute work or labour are classified as 'workers' and receive the benefits of for example the Equal Pay Act 1970, Sex Discrimination Act 1986 (SDA), Race Relations Act 1976 (RRA), Disability Discrimination Act 1995 (DDA), Employment Rights Act 1996 (ERA), ss 13–27, the National Minimum Wage Act 1999, and the Working Time Regulations 1998, etc. The definitions are at ERA 1996, s 230.

(c) Does the employee have sufficient service? An employee must have at least one year's continuous service in order to qualify to claim unfair dismissal, save for a dismissal on the ground of trade union membership activities, sex, disability and race discrimination, assertion of a statutory right and where a dismissal follows refusal by the employer to pay an employee who is suspended from work on medical grounds (when the employee need have been employed for only one month, in compliance with any law, regulation or code of practice providing for health and safety at work, ERA 1996, s 108(2)).

(d) Is the contract of employment lawful? The contract may be illegal, for example, if it has provisions in it which are intended to defraud the Inland Revenue.

(e) Is the employee employed by a person within the excluded categories? That is, overseas governments which have sovereign immunity, share fishermen, police, certain seamen.

(f) Is the employee over the normal retiring age for an employee holding the position he held? Or, if there is no normal retiring age, above 65 (ERA 1996, s 109(1)). The normal retiring age may be set out in the contract of employment or derived from practice in the establishment. Differential retiring ages for men and women are unlawful (SDA 1986).

(g) Has the employee excluded his rights to bring a claim by agreement? There are only strictly limited circumstances in which the employee can validly bargain away his rights. They are:

- where an ACAS Conciliation Officer has 'taken action' regarding the agreement, usually by negotiating a settlement of tribunal proceedings (see 5.3 below);

- where there is a valid compromise agreement in which the employee has received advice from an independent lawyer or a relevant independent adviser, ERA 1996, s203.

3.1.2   What service is continuous?

In general, if in a week an employee is not bound by a contract, continuity is broken so that the employee would have to start again to build up continuity (ERA 1996, ss 210–19). The contract subsists throughout the period of ordinary and additional maternity leave. There are, however, some 'bridging' rules which allow continuity to be maintained even though there is no subsisting contract of employment, that is where:

(a) there has been a temporary cessation of work: for example, a factory is subject to a short term closure due to lack of orders, a fire, explosion or a strike at the company's suppliers. It would cover seasonal absences in, for example, agriculture or hotel and catering. Whether the cessation is temporary is a question of fact, but in one case it lasted two years;

(b) the absence is taken by arrangement or custom: that is where it is understood that the employee will be taken back after a break or secondment;

(c) the employee is sick or injured: this can last only up to 26 weeks, unless the contract of employment subsists throughout the whole period of absence.

When employees are on strike, their continuity of service is not broken but the weeks on strike are not counted towards the computation of the period of service.

Normally, service with one employer cannot be added to service with another. There are, however, the following exceptions:

(a) where a trade, business or undertaking is transferred from one person to another. This does not apply where merely physical assets are sold, or the employing business is to be changed after sale beyond recognition;

(b) where an employee is taken into the employment of an associated employer. This is narrowly defined as a 'company of which the other (directly or indirectly) has control or if both are companies of which a third person (directly or indirectly) has control' (ERA 1996, s 231(4)). This cannot apply to local authorities or any institution other than a company. 'Control' here normally means voting control in a general meeting;

(c) where a personal employer dies and his personal representatives or trustees keep on the employee;

(d) where there is a change in the partners, personal representatives or trustees who employ the worker.

3.2 Key elements

The key elements in assessing whether there is a case of unfair dismissal are dismissal, reason for dismissal and reasonableness. Provided that the employee is qualified to bring a claim (and, generally, the onus of proof that he is excluded rests on the employer), in a claim that a dismissal is unfair:

(a) the employee must prove that he has been dismissed (ERA 1996, s 95);

(b) the employer must prove that he has dismissed the employee for one of the valid reasons, that is incapability, misconduct, contravention of a duty or restriction imposed by or under an enactment, redundancy or some other substantial reason for dismissal (ERA 1996, s 98(1) and (2));

(c) the tribunal must consider fairness but there is no burden of proof on either party on this issue (ERA 1996, s 98(4));

(d) the applicant must prove his loss which arises consequential on his dismissal (ERA 1996, ss 118–26).

(e) the employer must prove failure to mitigate and contributory fault.

3.2.1 Dismissal

There are three statutory species of dismissal.

(a) Direct dismissal – In order to establish a dismissal under statute, there must be unequivocal words of termination and a date must be set for the termination. Words uttered in the heat of the moment do not qualify: *Morton Sundour Fabrics Ltd v Shaw* (1967) 2 ITR 84 (a date for termination must either be set or be capable of being identified from the words of dismissal); *Tanner v Kean* [1978] IRLR 110 (the ending of a vitriolic attack on the employer with the words 'You're finished with me' was not an effective dismissal); (see, also, *J and J Stern v Simpson* [1983] IRLR 52; *Sovereign House Security Services Ltd v Savage* [1989] IRLR 115; *Kwik Fit (GB) Ltd v Lineham* [1992] IRLR 183); *Hogg v Dover College* [1990] ICR 39 (an employee may claim to be dismissed when one contract is terminated but he is offered another contract with the same employer).

(b) Expiry of a fixed term contract without its being renewed

(c) Constructive dismissal – resignation in reaction to a fundamental breach of contract by the employer such as a reduction in pay, change in job content or status, place of work, punishing the employee in a way which is out of proportion with the misconduct committed: *British Aircraft Corporation v Austin* [1978] IRLR 332 (it is an implied term that the employer will not make the life of the employee intolerable); *Western Excavating (ECC) Ltd v Sharp* [1978] QB 761 (the general test); *Woods v WM Car Services (Peterborough) Ltd* [1982] IRLR 413 (consistent attempts to vary the employee's contract may be a fundamental breach).

A constructive dismissal may still be justified as fair if the employer acted reasonably in all the circumstances (ERA 1978, s 95(1)).

The following terminations of the contract of employment do not qualify as dismissals:

(a) an agreed termination; see, for example, *Logan Salton v Durham CC* [1989] IRLR 99;

(b) a resignation (other than in reaction to a fundamental breach of contract by the employer);

(c) frustration of the contract by, for example, long-term sickness, or a period of imprisonment;

(d) termination by performance of a particular task in a 'task contract'.

3.2.2 Date

The effective date of termination (ERA 1996, s 97(1)–(4)) is important for several purposes including the qualifying period before a claim may be brought, the calculation date of a week's pay and the relevant age. The main outline rules are that the effective date of termination is:

(a) where an employee is dismissed with notice, the date on which the notice expires;

(b) where the dismissal is lawfully carried out without notice (by reason of the employee's gross misconduct), the date of that dismissal;

(c) where notice should by reason of the minimum notice periods in ERA 1996, s 86 be given longer than that notice which has in fact been given, the end of the period of proper minimum notice (this provision only applies for certain purposes such as the basic award of compensation);

(d) in the case of a fixed term contract, the date when that fixed term expires without being renewed under the same contract.

3.2.3 Reason

The reason for dismissal must be based on facts known to the employer at the date of dismissal and not those which came to light only after that date. An employee who has served for more than one year is entitled to written reasons for his dismissal. The following reasons are automatically unfair as reasons for dismissal:

(a) pregnancy, childbirth, maternity, ordinary, compulsory or additional maternity leave, parental leave or taking time off if for dependents (ERA 1996, ss 99, 106);

(b) trade union activities or membership or non-membership of a union (Trade Union and Labour Relations (Consolidation) Act 1992 (TULR(C)A), s 152);

(c) a conviction which is 'spent' under the Rehabilitation of Offenders Act 1974;

(d) a reason connected with a transfer of undertaking save where there are 'economic, technical or organisational reasons entailing changes in the workforce' (Transfer of Undertakings (Protection of Employment) Regulations 1981, reg 8);

(e) because the employee has made a public interest disclosure.

(f) for assertion of a statutory right (see *Mennell v Newell & Wright (Transport Contractors) Ltd* [1997] ICR 1039).

The employer may change the label he puts on the reason for dismissal, but not the facts underlying it. When employment is terminated on notice the tribunal can take into account the reasons both at the time when dismissal occurred and also when prior notice expires if different (*Parkinson v March Consulting Ltd* [1998] ICR 276).

The employment tribunal must take no account of events occurring subsequent to the dismissal or facts not known to the employer at the time of dismissal in dealing with liability (*W Devis and Sons v Atkins* [1977] AC 931, HL) but it can consider what occurs on an internal appeal (*West Midlands Cooperative Society Ltd v Tipton* [1986] ICR 192, HL). Further, it should consider all the circumstances when compensation falls to be assessed.

If there is more than one reason for dismissal, the employer does not have to select the principal reason and merely rely on that: for example, *Hotson v Wisbech Conservative Club* [1984] ICR 859 (it is improper at the employment tribunal hearing to change the reason from incapability to dishonesty); *Maund v Penwith DC* [1984] ICR 143 (onus of proof where the employee alleges that he was dismissed for trade union activities; it is still for the employer to prove the reason for dismissal); *Smith v City of Glasgow DC* [1987] IRLR 326 (if the employer seeks to rely on several reasons, he must either establish them all or show that the dismissal was justified solely on the reasons he can establish).

3.2.4 Reasonableness

The employment tribunal must decide whether the dismissal was fair or unfair on the basis of whether the employer behaved reasonably in all the circumstances in treating the reason or, if more than one, the principal reason of the employer as a sufficient reason for dismissal and having regard to the size and administrative resources of the employer's undertaking. Further,

(a) the tribunals do not encourage excessive use of guidelines since each case depends on its own merits;

(b) an improper procedure may or may not render a dismissal unfair, depending on the seriousness of the breach and all the circumstances of the case;

(c) natural justice is not a separate head of fairness (*Slater v Leicestershire HA* [1989] IRLR 16);

(d) the small size of the employer may mean that it does not have to achieve the same exacting standards as the large employer, but it does not excuse him from any procedure at all (*De Grasse v Stockwell Tool Ltd* [1992] IRLR 269);

(e) the failure to follow a contractual appeals procedure will not necessarily render the dismissal unfair (*Westminster CC v Cabaj* [1996] ICR 960).

3.3 Questions

This section sets an 'agenda' for questions to be asked in each type of unfair dismissal case. In setting them out in summary form, vital issues have had to be simplified. Readers should look in the standard works for further information (see Chapter 11).

3.3.1 Incompetence

(a) Has the employee been warned about his competence?

(b) Has the employee been given an opportunity to improve after a warning?

(c) Has the employer maintained a system of appraisal to monitor the employee's progress?

(d) If the employee is a probationer, has he been given a clear brief of what the job involves?

(e) Is the incompetence so serious that there is no need to warn the employee?

(f) Is the employee engaged in a special category of activities requiring a high degree of skill such as an express train driver in charge of hazardous loads, an airline pilot, a chemist researching new drugs (in which case, the employer may dismiss for a single act of incompetence because of the seriousness of the consequences)?

(g) Has the employer carried out his responsibility of giving the employee the necessary support and assistance to allow the employee to adapt to change?

(h) If the employee is incapable of carrying out his present job, is there a suitable alternative position available?

For example, *Cook v Thomas Linnell and Sons Ltd* [1977] ICR 770 ('When responsible employers genuinely come to the conclusion that over a reasonable period of time a manager is incompetent, we think it is some evidence that he is incompetent'); *Post Office v Mughal* [1977] IRLR 178 (emphasises the need for reasonable appraisal of the employee before dismissal); *Taylor v Alidair Ltd* [1978] IRLR 82 (airline pilot fairly dismissed for bad landing which caused serious damage to aircraft); *Winterhalter Gastronom Ltd v Webb* [1973] IRLR 120 (the need for warning; evidence of incompetence in poor sales record).

3.3.2 Ill health

(a) Is the employee a 'key worker' for whose work it is difficult to provide cover?

(b) Has the employer taken an informed view of the employee's health based on proper medical information?

(c) Has the employer consulted the employee for his own views on his health?

(d) Is the contract one which clearly requires robust good health such as work on an oil production platform in the North Sea?

(e) Is there a provision on or relating to absence for sickness in the contract of employment or collective agreement?

(f) Has the employee had a series of intermittent absences which cause great difficulties for the employer in seeking to redistribute his work or provide cover?

(g) Has the employer given appropriate warnings to the employee that his employment might be brought to an end?

(h) Should the employee be examined by an independent specialist (as well as a GP, or the company doctor)?

(i) What is the likely duration of the employee's illness?

(j) Does the employee's illness make him a potential danger to fellow employees?

(k) Could continued employment of the employee risk a breach of the law?

(l) Was the illness a result of an accident at work (in which case the employer may be required to show extra sympathy)?

(m) Is there a (possibly sedentary) job available which the employer could carry out?

(n) Has the contract been frustrated through a long period of sickness absence?

Where there is no medical evidence to support frequent short term self-certificated absences, the employee should be asked to see a doctor to consider whether medical treatment is necessary. If it appears that there is no good reason for the absences, the matter should be treated as a disciplinary matter.

It is necessary to consider the terms of the Disability Discrimination Act 1995 including the need to make reasonable adjustments.

The ACAS Handbook *Discipline at Work* states that in general 'the employer is not expected to create a special job for the employee concerned, nor to be a medical expert, but to take action on the basis of the medical evidence': for example, *East Lindsey DC v Daubney* [1977] ICR 566 (emphasises the need for consultation with the employee); *Hutchinson v Enfield Rolling Mills Ltd* [1981] IRLR 318 (the employer may look behind a medical note if he has evidence that the employee is malingering); *International Sports Co Ltd v Thomson* [1980] IRLR 340 (intermittent absences – see, also, *Rolls Royce Ltd v Walpole* [1980] IRLR 43); *Leonard v Fergus and Haynes Civil Engineering Ltd* [1979] IRLR 235 (the terms of the contract for a steel fixer made it clear that good health was required for work on a North Sea oil platform; dismissal fair); *Walton v TAC Construction Materials Ltd* [1981] IRLR 357 (dismissal of heroin addict held to be fair).

3.3.3 Misconduct

Disobedience to orders and instructions

(a) Is the instruction given by the employer within the contract of employment, and is it lawful and reasonable in all the circumstances? (Check the written statement of terms, collective agreement, works rules, custom and practice, etc.)

(b) Were the relevant rules properly made known to the employee (but this is probably not necessary when it should be obvious, for example, drunkenness, fighting)?

(c) Do the rules make it clear that an employee in breach will be dismissed?

Note the ACAS Code of Practice on Disciplinary Practice and Procedures in Employment, para 5:

> ... if they are to be fully effective, the rules and procedures need to be accepted as reasonable by both those who are to be covered by them and by those who operate them.

The ACAS Handbook states that company rules should cover matters such as timekeeping, absence, health and safety, discipline at work and use of company facilities.

The rules should be applied irrespective of sex, marital status, race, disability and the length of service of the employee (ACAS Handbook). If there are rules and the employee acts in breach of the rules, the dismissal is only likely to be unfair if:

(a) the rule has no relevance to the employment;

(b) the rule is ambiguous in its terms;

(c) the punishment is too serious for the 'crime' committed;

(d) the employer has ignored the employee's years of good service and the employee has been dismissed for one or two minor breaches;

(e) the employer has been inconsistent in treatment between different employees, but to prove this:

- employees must over a period have been led to believe that certain categories of conduct would be overlooked or at least not dealt with by dismissal;

- evidence in relation to the other cases must support the inference that the employer's given reason for dismissal was not the real reason;

- the circumstances in the other case(s) must be truly parallel;

(f) the employer has not considered the individual case, but has just imposed a blanket policy of dismissal;

(g) the employee is faced with a 'stale' allegation.

On the relevance of the lawfulness of an instruction, see *Farrant v Woodroffe School* [1998] ICR 185.

Particular examples of misconduct are as follows:

(a) absenteeism: *City of Edinburgh DC v Stephen* [1977] IRLR 135;

(b) abusive behaviour: *Rosenthal v Louis Butler Ltd* [1972] IRLR 39;

(c) computer 'hacking': *Denco Ltd v Joinson* [1991] IRLR 63;

(d) disloyalty: entering into competition with employer – *Laughton and Hawley v Bapp Industrial Supplies Ltd* [1986] IRLR 245;

(e) drinking: *Distillers Co (Bottling Services) Ltd v Gardner* [1982] IRLR 47; *Dairy Produce Packers Ltd v Beverstock* [1981] IRLR 265;

(f) fighting: *CA Parsons and Co v McLoughlin* [1978] IRLR 65;

(g) taking holiday without permission: *Brandon and Goold v Murphy Bros* [1983] IRLR 54;

(h) refusal to co-operate with employers: *Retarded Children's Aid Society v Day* [1978] ICR 437;

(i) refusal to work overtime: *Martin v Solus Schall* [1979] IRLR 7;

(j) sexual offences committed outside work: *Wiseman v Salford CC* [1981] IRLR 202;

(k) smoking: *Unkles v Milanda Bread Co* [1973] IRLR 76;

(l) theft: *British Leyland (UK) Ltd v Swift* [1981] IRLR 91.

3.3.4 Offences

(a) Was the offence committed at work or outside?

(b) If it was committed outside work, does it at least have an effect on the work: for example, is it an offence of dishonesty and is the employee in a position of trust? The ACAS Code of Practice, para 15(c) asks whether such an offence 'makes the individual unsuitable for his or her type of work or unacceptable to other employees'.

(c) Has the employee concealed from the employer criminal convictions before he joined? (See the Rehabilitation of Offenders Act 1974.)

(d) Has there been a reasonable investigation? (But this is not normally necessary where the employee admits his guilt or makes a tacit admission.)

(e) Has the employer carried out an investigation into the misconduct reasonably quickly without rushing it?

An employee charged with or convicted of an offence should not automatically be disciplined or dismissed. The employer must have regard to the employment implications alone. He does not, however, have to wait until a prosecution has been completed before deciding whether to dismiss. The internal investigation is entirely separate from the police investigation and any decision by the Crown Prosecution Service to bring charges against the employee.

3.3.5 Standard of proof

The degree of proof required of misconduct is:

> ... a reasonable suspicion amounting to a belief in the guilt of the employee of that misconduct at that time ... First of all, there must be established by the employer the fact of that belief; that the employer did believe it. Secondly, that the employer had in his mind reasonable grounds on which to sustain that belief. And, thirdly, ... that the employer at the stage at which he formed that belief on those grounds ... had carried out as much investigation into the matter as was reasonable in all the circumstances of the case.

(*BHS Ltd v Burchell* [1978] IRLR 379, *per* Arnold J). This should not be applied as a mantra in every case (*Boys and Girls Welfare Society v Macdonald* [1997] ICR 693; see, also, *Wilson v Ethicon Ltd* [2000] IRLR 4; *Haddon v Van Den Bergh Foods Ltd* [1999] IRLR 672).

Employers must not form their belief hastily without making reasonable enquiries (*Weddel and Co Ltd v Tepper* [1980] IRLR 96; *Whitbread & Co v Thomas* [1988] IRLR 43).

Where the finger of suspicion points to one or other of two employees both may be dismissed (*Monie v Coral Racing Ltd* [1980] IRLR 464; *Parr v Whitbread plc* [1990] IRLR 39). The question to be asked is whether there were 'solid and sensible grounds on which the employer could reasonably infer or suspect dishonesty'. For example, *Harris (Ipswich) Ltd v Harrison* [1978] IRLR 382 (a dismissal may be fair even though a criminal court acquits the employee); *McLaren v National Coal Board* [1987] ICR 410; [1988] IRLR 215, CA (the employer cannot – even in the special circumstances of the miners' strike – dismiss an employee merely because he has been convicted of an offence); *Moore v C&A Modes* [1981] IRLR 71 (dismissal of a shop assistant who stole from a nearby shop held fair); *Linfood Cash and Carry v Thomson* [1989] IRLR 235 (use of informers).

3.3.6 Contravention of statutory duty or restriction

This heading is very rarely found in practice, but the employer may rely on it when, for example, an employee failed the statutory qualification as hearing aid dispenser, or a driver was disqualified from driving.

3.3.7 Redundancy

(a) Has the employer selected the employee for redundancy:
- for an inadmissible reason, that is, membership of, or activities at an appropriate time in, an independent trade union or refusal to join a trade union: ERA 1996, s 105 and TULR(C)A 1992, s 153?
- unreasonably in all the circumstances: ERA 1996, s 98(4)?

(b) Did the employer adopt objective selection criteria such as comparative attendance records, last in first out?

(c) Were the selection criteria fairly applied?

(d) Were employees warned in advance about redundancies?

(e) Were the trade union(s) and employees consulted about ways to avoid redundancies and the selection procedure? See, in the case of recognised unions, TULR(C)A 1992, ss 188–92 on the duty of an employer to consult recognised trade unions or employee representatives over redundancies (*Mugford v Midland Bank plc* [1997] ICR 399).

(f) Has the employer taken reasonable steps to find a suitable alternative job for the employee?

(g) Has the employer made clear the alternative job being offered and given the employee a reasonable time in which to make up his mind whether to accept it?

(h) Has the employer informed the employee that he will have a trial period in which to decide whether to accept the alternative job? (*Elliot v Richard Stump Ltd* [1987] IRLR 215.)

(i) If the employee may have vacancies in the future, has he put the employee on a list of persons from whom such vacancies may be filled?

3.3.8 Some other substantial reasons

There is deemed to be some other substantial reason for dismissal where:

(a) the employee was dismissed after being taken on as a temporary replacement for an employee away on maternity leave or under medical suspension; ERA 1996, s 106;

(b) a dismissal arises consequent on a transfer of undertaking and was
for an 'economic, technical or organisational reason entailing
changes in the workforce': Transfer of Undertakings (Protection
of Employment) Regulations 1981, reg 8(2).

Reorganisation

This is one of the categories most commonly found under the other
substantial reason rubric. The questions are:

(a) is there a 'pressing business reason' for the reorganisation? (NB
the employer must produce evidence of this reason.)

(b) has the employer carried out a reasonable degree of consultation
with the employee before imposing changes?

(c) what evidence can be adduced of the need to reorganise?

Note *Chubb Fire Security Ltd v Harper* [1983] IRLR 311 (it may be
possible to balance the advantages for the employer of the
reorganisation as opposed to the disadvantages to the employee);
Hollister v NFU [1979] ICR 542 (employee dismissed for refusing to
sign a new contract which would have substantially cut his income;
held to be fair dismissal even though the employer had not consulted
the employee beforehand); *Orr v Vaughan* [1981] IRLR 63 (the
employer must act on reasonable information reasonably acquired as
to his business needs); *RS Components Ltd v Irwin* [1973] ICR 535
(employees dismissed for refusing to sign restrictive covenant, held:
fair); *St John of God (Care Services) Ltd v Brooks* [1992] IRLR 546 (the
central issue is not whether the new terms offered were reasonable,
but whether the employer was acting reasonably in dismissing for the
refusal itself); *Catamaran Cruisers Ltd v Williams* [1994] IRLR 386.

Dismissal on expiry of fixed term contract

(a) Was the fixed term contract adopted for a genuine purpose?

(b) Was the purpose made clear to the employee?

(c) Had the purpose for which the contract was adopted ceased?

Note *North Yorkshire CC v Fay* [1985] IRLR 247 (a vital question is
whether the fixed term contract was adopted for a genuine purpose);
Terry v East Sussex CC [1976] ICR 536 (has the employee to his
knowledge been employed for a temporary purpose?).

Miscellaneous cases

Dobie v Burns International Security Services (UK) Ltd [1984] ICR 812 (dismissal at the behest of a major client held to be fair); *Harper v National Coal Board* [1980] IRLR 260 (employee had epileptic fits); *Saunders v Scottish National Camps Association Ltd* [1980] IRLR 174 (homosexual employed at children's holiday camp); *Skyrail Oceanic v Coleman* [1980] ICR 596 (employee was going to marry a man who worked for a rival travel agent: held unfair because no warning of dismissal); *Turner v Vestric Ltd* [1980] ICR 528 (breakdown in relationships between employees, but employer must make reasonable efforts to improve relationships).

3.3.9 Pregnancy

(a) Is the employee entitled to return to work? Has she complied with the various notification requirements?

(b) Is the employee capable of adequately carrying out her work?

(c) Can the employee carry on her work without breaking the law, for example, s 75 of the Factories Act 1961 which requires that employers take women off jobs when so advised by the Employment Medical Advice Service?

Note *Grimsby Carpet Co Ltd v Bedford* [1987] IRLR 438 (in order to render a dismissal potentially fair, the incapacity need not arise from the pregnancy itself, but may be caused by a connected matter such as a miscarriage or sickness); *Brown v Stockton on Tees BC* [1988] ICR 410; *Clayton v Viggers* [1990] IRLR 177; *Webb v EMO Air Cargo (UK) Ltd* [1994] ICR 77.

3.3.10 Strike or lock-out

(a) If the action was official, has the employer dismissed all those engaged in the strike or other industrial action at the same time as the employee and not re-engaged any of them within three months?

(b) Was the employee participating in the strike or other industrial action at the time of dismissal, or did the employee not work because he was genuinely sick or on holiday?

(c) If the employee was dismissed during a lock-out, have all those employees with a direct interest in the dispute in contemplation or furtherance of which the lock-out was called been dismissed?

(d) If the employer has not dismissed all those on strike or engaging in industrial action, the employment tribunal has to consider whether the dismissal was reasonable in the normal way, taking as the reason for dismissal the reason why that employee was dismissed and others were retained.

Section 237 of TULR(C)A 1992 renders it possible to dismiss any employee taking part in unofficial strike action even though not all such employees are dismissed. The employment tribunal has no jurisdiction in such a case. Where the dismissal was in the course of official industrial action, the employer may not dismiss during the first eight weeks of the action or thereafter if the employee dismissed had stopped taking the action or the 'employer had not taken such procedural steps as would have been reasonable for the purposes of resolving the dispute to which the protected industrial action relates' (s 238A of TULR(C)A 1992 amended by Employment Relations Act 1999).

3.3.11 Closed shop

It is unfair to dismiss someone because they would not join a closed shop union. Such a dismissal is, like a dismissal for trade union membership or activities, automatically unfair.

3.3.12 Transfer of undertaking

(a) Is the reason or principal reason for the dismissal an economic, technical or organisational reason entailing changes in the workforce of the transferor or transferee? Otherwise, the dismissal will be automatically unfair: *Ibex Trading Co Ltd v Walton* [1994] ICR 907. See, also Bowers, J, *Bowers on Employment Law*, 3rd edn, 2000; Elias, P and Bowers, J, *Transfer of Undertakings: The Legal Pitfalls*, 5th edn, 1995; Mead, M, *Unfair Dismissal*, 5th edn 1994, pp 313–34.

3.4 Procedure

In *Polkey v A E Dayton Services Ltd* [1987] IRLR 503, Lord Mackay of Clashfern said (para 28):

> ... in the case of misconduct, the employer will normally not act reasonably unless he investigates the complaint of misconduct fully and fairly and hears whatever the employee wishes to say in his defence or in explanation or

mitigation ... It is quite a different matter if the tribunal is able to conclude that the employer himself, at the time of the dismissal, acted reasonably in taking the view that, in the exceptional circumstances of the particular case, the procedural steps normally appropriate would have been futile, could not have altered the decision to dismiss and therefore could be dispensed with. In such a case, the test of reasonableness under s 57(3) may be satisfied.

It is not permissible to ask on the question of liability for unfair dismissal whether if the employer had carried out the proper procedures the result would have been the same, although this will be relevant to the amount of compensation to be awarded (*Polkey v A E Dayton Services Ltd* [1987] IRLR 503; *Duffy v Yeomans and Partners* [1995] ICR 1; *Wolseley Centers Ltd v Simmons* [1994] ICR 503; see 3.5.3 below).

Where several employees are engaged in an alleged act of misconduct, their cases must be considered separately, although if different punishments are meted out, the employer's decision may be attacked on the grounds of inconsistency of treatment.

3.4.1 Warnings

(a) ACAS Code of Practice: in the case of minor offences there should be a formal oral warning followed by a written warning and then a final written warning which should specify that recurrence of the offence may/will lead to dismissal.

(b) Warnings should be removed from an employee's record after a reasonable time, usually six months for minor warnings and one year for final warnings (ACAS Handbook).

(c) A warning will not be necessary where:

- the conduct, such as violence is clearly serious misconduct;
- the disciplinary rules are so clear as to constitute a warning of dismissal in themselves (*Meridian Ltd v Gomersall* [1977] ICR 597);
- the employee knew or ought to know that by his action he was putting his job in jeopardy.

Note *East Hertfordshire DC v Boyten* [1977] IRLR 347 where it was decided that if the employer has followed procedures agreed between union and employer, it will be difficult for the employee to show that the procedure was unfair.

3.4.2 Investigation and hearing

(a) The ACAS Handbook states that in cases which appear to involve serious misconduct a brief period of suspension (with pay unless the contract provides otherwise) should be considered pending the investigation.

(b) ACAS Code of Practice, para 11: before a decision is made or penalty imposed the individual should be interviewed and given the opportunity to state his or her case and should be advised of any rights under the procedure including the statutory right to be accompanied.

In general:

(c) the employee should know in advance the case he has to meet;

(d) in most cases, however, the employee does not have to be given the opportunity formally to cross-examine witnesses to the misconduct alleged;

(e) the hearing body should act in good faith and no members should have been involved earlier in the disciplinary process;

(f) the hearing should take place as soon as possible after the alleged misconduct has been discovered;

(g) the employee should have the right to be represented;

(h) where a union official is the subject of discipline, no disciplinary action beyond an oral warning should be taken until the case has been discussed with the union;

(i) it is good practice to adjourn a hearing before a decision is taken to allow proper consideration of all matters raised.

Note *Khanum v Mid Glamorgan AHA* [1979] ICR 40 (a dismissal was not rendered unfair because the employee did not have an opportunity to cross-examine witnesses against her); *Marley Homecare Ltd v Dutton* [1981] IRLR 380 (a dismissal was unfair where an employee was dismissed seven days after committing a breach of till procedure; the delay meant that she was unable to identify the relevant incident when questioned about it); *Clark v Civil Aviation Authority* [1991] IRLR 412.

3.4.3 Appeals

(a) The employee should be informed of his right to appeal and the right to be represented at that appeal.

(b) The appeal body should be composed of different persons to those who decided to dismiss, wherever possible.

(c) The employment tribunal can take into account what occurs at an appeal even though it takes place after the effective date of dismissal itself.

(d) The employer should specify clearly any time limit within which the appeal should be lodged.

(e) Appeals should be heard speedily.

(f) The employee should have an opportunity to comment on any new event.

See *Whitbread plc v Mills* [1988] ICR 776: where the appeal takes the form of a re-hearing, faults in an initial hearing may be corrected on appeal.

3.5 Remedies

3.5.1 Reinstatement

This is an order that the employee be put back in the same position he held before dismissal, with all benefits paid to him which he lost between the date of dismissal and the date of reinstatement. In deciding whether to make the order, the employment tribunal must at least consider the following matters:

(a) whether the applicant wishes to be reinstated;

(b) whether it is practicable for the employer to comply with such an order; and

(c) whether the applicant caused or contributed to some extent to the dismissal: although such a finding is not an absolute bar to an order being made: ERA 1996, s 116.

Employment tribunals have decided against reinstatement where:

(a) the employee has shown in the course of the proceedings that she distrusts the employer (*Nothman v London Borough of Barnet (No 2)* [1980] IRLR 65);

(b) there has been a redundancy situation affecting the employee's position following the dismissal (*Trusler v Lummus Co Ltd* [1972] IRLR 35);

(c) it would lead to industrial unrest (*Langston v AUEW (No 2)* [1974] ICR 510);

(d) the employee would be insufficiently employed (*Tayside Regional Council v McIntosh* [1982] IRLR 272);

(e) the employer is small and the parties would have to be in 'close personal relationships with each other' (*Enessy Co SA v Minoprio* [1978] IRLR 489).

An employment tribunal may, however, order reinstatement even though the employer:

(a) claims that there is no existing vacancy (*Electronic Data Processing Ltd v Wright* [1986] IRLR 8); or

(b) has a lingering belief in the employee's dishonesty (*The Boots Company Ltd v Lees-Collier* [1986] ICR 728).

It is not sufficient for the employer merely to show that reinstatement is inexpedient: *Port of London Authority v Payne* [1994] IRLR 9; see, also, *Cold Drawn Tubes v Middleton* [1992] ICR 318).

3.5.2 Re-engagement

A re-engagement order puts the employee back to work for the same employer or an associated employer but not in the same position or on the same terms and conditions as before the dismissal. Rather, it is in a job which is as far as is reasonably practicable as favourable as the previous position, or other suitable employment. The terms of the re-engagement order are within the discretion of the employment tribunal.

If the employer refuses to comply with an order for reinstatement or re-engagement, the employment tribunal may make an additional award of loss suffered.

The employer will not be subject to an additional award if he proves that it was not reasonably practicable to comply with the reinstatement or re-engagement order, and in deciding this issue the employment tribunal may take account of all relevant facts both before and after the order was made.

3.5.3 Compensation

(a) The basic award consists of:
- one-and-a-half week's pay for each year which consists wholly of weeks in which the employee was over the age of 41;
- one week's pay for each year which consists wholly of weeks in which the employee was over the age of 22 but below 41;
- one-half week's pay for each year which consists wholly of weeks in which the employee was below 22.

Note: there is a maximum ceiling of 20 years' employment to be counted, which, depending on the age of the employee, may make a multiplier of 30 week's pay.

- There is a maximum of the week's pay of £240 (subject to yearly increase in accordance with the retail price index every September);

- the week's gross pay at the date of dismissal is taken as the multiplier;

- any redundancy pay is set off against a basic award, but there is a set off only *if* the Employment Tribunal (ET) finds that the dismissal was by reason of redundancy and not some other substantial reason: *Boorman v Allmakes Ltd* [1995] IRLR 553. Any excess redundancy pay over and above the statutory limit is taken as the compensatory award;

- where the employee is over 64, the amount of basic award is reduced by one 12th for each month of that last year.

(b) The compensatory award is such compensation as is just and equitable having regard to the loss suffered as a result of the dismissal: ERA 1996, s 124. This is subject to a maximum of, at present, £51,700, but offers the employment tribunal a very wide discretion within that limit. There is no maximum limit in cases of sex, disability or race discrimination or under the Public Interest Disclosure Act 1998 or health and safety dismissals (s 100). See ERA 1996, s 124.

Compensation is normally made up of:

(a) loss of earnings between dismissal and the employment tribunal hearing, subject to deduction for anything earned during this period; this element can usually be easily calculated;

(b) future loss of earnings: the employment tribunal must take a view of the likely period during which the applicant will be out of work or earning less than in his previous employment; the employment tribunal considers what is likely to happen on the balance of probabilities;

(c) loss of fringe benefits: see list of possible benefits at 2.1 above; for valuation of loss of car see AA or RAC tables (contained in Korn, A, *Compensation for Dismissal*, 2nd edn, 1997);

(d) expenses of looking for alternative work as an employee or as a self employed person;

(e) loss of pensions: this is a complex calculation and the amount is usually based on the government actuary's department table (see also HMSO booklet 'Compensation for Loss of Pension Rights');

(f) loss of employment protection rights: a conventional sum of about £200 for the employee who will have to build up continuous service in another employment to claim statutory employment rights.

The Court of Appeal has stressed that tribunals should 'paint the picture with a broad brush' (*Fougere v Phoenix Motor Co Ltd* [1976] IRLR 259).

(a) Contributory fault: The basic and compensatory awards may be reduced if 'the dismissal is to any extent caused or contributed to by any action of the complainant': ERA 1996, s 122(2) and s 123(6). In an extreme case, the compensation may be reduced to nil (for example, *Chaplin v Rawlinson* [1991] ICR 553). Participation in industrial action cannot, in itself, amount to contributory fault (*Tracey v Crosville Wales Ltd* [1997] ICR 862).

(b) The employee is under a duty to mitigate his loss, just as at common law: ERA 1996, s 123. What is reasonable mitigation is a question of fact in each case. In general, the employee need not take the first available job but after a reasonable period should take a position at a lower rate of pay. The employment tribunal calculates how long the employee would be out of work if he had taken reasonable steps to mitigate his loss. The onus of proof of lack of mitigation rests on the employer (*Fyfe v Scientific Furnishings Ltd* [1989] IRLR 331). In most cases, an employer will not be criticised for refusing another position with the employer who has just dismissed him. There are some situations where the duty to mitigate is not applicable, that is where there is a pay in lieu of notice or liquidate damages clause: *Abrahams v Performing Rights Society* [1996] IRLR 486 and *Cerebus Software Ltd v Rowley* (2001) not yet reported, CA.

(c) If the employee has received Job Seeker's Allowance or income support between the date of his dismissal and the hearing of the employment tribunal, the DSS may recoup the payments made out of the award of compensation. Where the case is settled, these recoupment provisions do not apply as there has been no award of compensation.

The following points should be noted regarding compensation:

(a) If the employee suffers no injustice because of his dismissal, he may receive no award from the employment tribunal at all, and the tribunal will ask the question whether it would have made any difference if the proper procedures had been put into effect. If so, what would have been the difference to the result (for example, *Britool Ltd v Roberts* [1993] IRLR 481; *Wolseley Centers Ltd v Simmons* [1994] ICR 503; *Dunlop Ltd v Farrell* [1993] ICR 885).

(b) The burden of proving loss and that he has mitigated his loss is on the applicant, while the employer has to prove contributory fault.

(c) If the employee might have been fairly dismissed in the near future, for example, if the employer had given him further warnings or a proper hearing, the employment tribunal may make an award only up to the time when it considers he might have been fairly dismissed, and/or reflecting the chance that if he had been properly consulted and/or warned he could not have been dismissed.

(d) An employment tribunal may award little or no compensation in the case of a dismissal which was unfair by reason of faulty procedure only if it is satisfied that if the proper procedure had been adopted the employers would have fairly reached the same result.

(e) There is a difference in terminology between compensation for unfair dismissal and damages for wrongful dismissal at common law.

(f) In general, an *ex gratia* payment by an employer designed to cover loss of earnings or to go towards unfair dismissal compensation will be deducted from an award, although there are exceptional cases where this does not occur. See *Digital Equipment Co. Ltd v Clements* [1996] ICR 829, *Digital Equipment Co Ltd v Clements (No 2)* [1998] IRLR 134 and *Heggie v Uniroyal Englebert Tyres Ltd* [1999] IRLR 802.

(g) Where a dismissal arises from sex, disability or race discrimination any award under the SDA 1975, DDA 1995 or RRA 1976 is set off against the compensatory award (s 126 of the Employment Rights Act 1996).

(h) The ET makes a reduction for contributory fault and then applies the statutory maximum. Thus, if the employee would lose £120,000 but was 50 per cent responsible for dismissal, he is entitled to the maximum of £51,700, and not half of that maximum, that is £25,850.

(i) The ET may hear evidence and submissions on contributory fault when considering 'liability' or in a separate compensation hearing (see Chapter 6). It is important to clarify with the tribunal at the outset of the hearing which course is to be adopted in the particular case.

(j) No reduction in the compensatory award can be made if the misconduct is discovered after the dismissal, but the rule is to the opposite effect in the case of the basic award.

(k) There is no limit on compensation in cases of sex, disability or race discrimination or for public interest disclosures. On the order for the application of excess payments, see *Digital Equipment Co Ltd v Clements (No 2)* [1998] ICR 258.

See *Addison v Babcock FATA* [1987] ICR 45 – in general, an employee is not entitled to both pay in lieu of notice and a compensatory award to cover the same period (see, also, *Horizon Holidays Ltd v Grassi* [1987] ICR 851); *Bessenden Properties Ltd v Corness* [1974] IRLR 338 where the general test for mitigation is laid down as follows:

If the complainant had no hope of recovering compensation from anybody else and if he had consulted merely his own interests and had acted reasonably in all the circumstances, would he have accepted the (alternative) job in mitigation of the loss which he had suffered?

3.5.4 Ready reckoner

For calculating the number of weeks' pay due in basic award and redundancy payment.

AGE (years)	SERVICE (years) 2	3	4	5	6	7	8	9	10	11	12	13	14	15	16	17	18	19	20
20	1	1	1	1	—														
21	1	1½	1½	1½	1½	—													
22	1	1½	2	2	2	2	—												
23	1½	2	2½	3	3	3	3	—											
24	2	2½	3	3½	4	4	4	4	—										
25	2	3	3½	4	4½	5	5	5	5	—									
26	2	3	4	4½	5	5½	6	6	6	6	—								
27	2	3	4	5	5½	6	6½	7	7	7	7	—							
28	2	3	4	5	6	6½	7	7½	8	8	8	8	—						
29	2	3	4	5	6	7	7½	8	8½	9	9	9	9	—					
30	2	3	4	5	6	7	8	8½	9	9½	10	10	10	10	—				
31	2	3	4	5	6	7	8	9	9½	10	10½	11	11	11	11	—			
32	2	3	4	5	6	7	8	9	10	10½	11	11½	12	12	12	12	—		
33	2	3	4	5	6	7	8	9	10	11	11½	12	12½	13	13	13	13	—	
34	2	3	4	5	6	7	8	9	10	11	12	12½	13	13½	14	14	14	14	—
35	2	3	4	5	6	7	8	9	10	11	12	13	13½	14	14½	15	15	15	15
36	2	3	4	5	6	7	8	9	10	11	12	13	14	14½	15	15½	16	16	16
37	2	3	4	5	6	7	8	9	10	11	12	13	14	15	15½	16	16½	17	17
38	2	3	4	5	6	7	8	9	10	11	12	13	14	15	16	16½	17	17½	18
39	2	3	4	5	6	7	8	9	10	11	12	13	14	15	16	17	17½	18	18½
40	2	3	4	5	6	7	8	9	10	11	12	13	14	15	16	17	18	18½	19
41	2	3	4	5	6	7	8	9	10	11	12	13	14	15	16	17	18	19	19½
42	2½	3½	4½	5½	6½	7½	8½	9½	10½	11½	12½	13½	14½	15½	16½	17½	18½	19½	20½
43	3	4	5	6	7	8	9	10	11	12	13	14	15	16	17	18	19	20	21
44	3	4½	5½	6½	7½	8½	9½	10½	11½	12½	13½	14½	15½	16½	17½	18½	19½	20½	21½
45	3	4½	6	7	8	9	10	11	12	13	14	15	16	17	18	19	20	21	22
46	3	4½	6	7½	8½	9½	10½	11½	12½	13½	14½	15½	16½	17½	18½	19½	20½	21½	22½
47	3	4½	6	7½	9	10	11	12	13	14	15	16	17	18	19	20	21	22	23
48	3	4½	6	7½	9	10½	11½	12½	13½	14½	15½	16½	17½	18½	19½	20½	21½	22½	23½
49	3	4½	6	7½	9	10½	12	13	14	15	16	17	18	19	20	21	22	23	24
50	3	4½	6	7½	9	10½	12	13½	14½	15½	16½	17½	18½	19½	20½	21½	22½	23½	24½
51	3	4½	6	7½	9	10½	12	13½	15	16	17	18	19	20	21	22	23	24	25
52	3	4½	6	7½	9	10½	12	13½	15	16½	17½	18½	19½	20½	21½	22½	23½	24½	25½
53	3	4½	6	7½	9	10½	12	13½	15	16½	18	19	20	21	22	23	24	25	26
54	3	4½	6	7½	9	10½	12	13½	15	16½	18	19½	20½	21½	22½	23½	24½	25½	26½
55	3	4½	6	7½	9	10½	12	13½	15	16½	18	19½	21	22	23	24	25	26	27
56	3	4½	6	7½	9	10½	12	13½	15	16½	18	19½	21	22½	23½	24½	25½	26½	27½
57	3	4½	6	7½	9	10½	12	13½	15	16½	18	19½	21	22½	24	25	26	27	28
58	3	4½	6	7½	9	10½	12	13½	15	16½	18	19½	21	22½	24	25½	26½	27½	28½
59	3	4½	6	7½	9	10½	12	13½	15	16½	18	19½	21	22½	24	25½	27	28	29
60	3	4½	6	7½	9	10½	12	13½	15	16½	18	19½	21	22½	24	25½	27	28½	29½
61	3	4½	6	7½	9	10½	12	13½	15	16½	18	19½	21	22½	24	25½	27	28½	30
62	3	4½	6	7½	9	10½	12	13½	15	16½	18	19½	21	22½	24	25½	27	28½	30
63	3	4½	6	7½	9	10½	12	13½	15	16½	18	19½	21	22½	24	25½	27	28½	30
64	3	4½	6	7½	9	10½	12	13½	15	16½	18	19½	21	22½	24	25½	27	28½	30
SERVICE (years)	2	3	4	5	6	7	8	9	10	11	12	13	14	15	16	17	18	19	20

4 Employment Tribunals

4.1 Employment tribunal

The employment tribunal is normally composed of a legally qualified chairman of at least seven years' professional experience and two lay members, one representing employers' organisations and the other the trade unions or a professional association. The tribunal may decide a case by a majority.

Discrimination claims

In a claim for sex discrimination, at least one member of each sex should sit on the panel, and in race discrimination cases a person with 'special knowledge or experience of relations between persons of different racial groups in the employment field' (as certified by the Lord Chancellor) should sit.

'Two-legged' tribunals

If both parties consent, a tribunal may consist of just two persons. Then the chairman would have a casting vote. A chairman may sit alone to hear all interlocutory applications except for pre-hearing review.

Chairman sitting alone

A chairman may sit alone to deal with interlocutory applications, employees' rights on insolvency, unlawful deduction claims under the Pt II of the Employment Rights Act 1996 (ERA) and the contractual jurisdiction of the employment tribunal.

Administrative structure

The administrative head of the employment tribunals is the President, at present HH Judge John Prophet. He is formally responsible for the selection of chairman, the sitting of tribunals and formal directions as to their sitting. Each Regional Office has an Assistant Secretary of Tribunals who is responsible for registering claims and in whose name correspondence goes out on interlocutory matters. An unqualified clerk sits in at each tribunal hearing for all or part of the hearing. He administers the oath, and keeps a record of witnesses and exhibits.

4.1.1 Legal aid and assistance

Legal aid is not available for representation before the employment tribunal (save in Scotland) but some free legal advice may be available through the Legal Services Commission. Some companies offer legal expenses insurance to cover unfair dismissal claims and many employee relations consultants offer such representation as part of their overall service.

CRE, EOC and DRC

The Commission for Racial Equality (CRE), Equal Opportunities Commission (EOC) or Disability Rights Commission (DRC) may assist an applicant with advice and representation in appropriate cases within their respective remits. They will provide help where a question of principle is raised on the facts of the case, or it is unreasonable, having regard to the complexity of the case, to expect the individual to proceed unaided. The respective discrimination commissions must respond to such an application within two months of its receipt.

Unrepresented parties

The tribunals were intended to have informal procedures in which representation by lawyers would not be necessary. About two-thirds of applicants and one-half of respondents are not represented by lawyers. Expert assistance is often, however, provided to applicants by trade unions, Citizens Advice Bureaux, the Free Representation Unit and Law Centres, and to respondents by trade associations or employment protection consultants. It should be possible to bring or defend proceedings in the employment tribunal without legal representation, and most chairmen will help an unrepresented applicant to understand the procedure and deal with such mysterious processes as examination and cross-examination. (See Bowers, J, Brown, D and Mead, G, *Employment Tribunal Practice and Procedure*, 2000.)

4.2 Commencing proceedings

An Originating Application starts proceedings in the employment tribunal. The official printed Form IT1 (see Chapter 9) is available from the Central Office of Employment Tribunals (COET), Regional Office of Employment Tribunals (ROET), most Citizens Advice Bureaux and Job Centres. It is not absolutely necessary to use the form, provided that the applicant states in writing:

(a) his name and address;

(b) the names and addresses of the respondent(s); and

(c) the details of his complaint and the remedy sought by him.

There are no tribunal fees to pay in bringing or defending a claim.

4.2.1 Presenting the application

Send the originating application to the Secretary of Employment Tribunals, Central Office of Employment Tribunals at 100 Southgate Street, Bury St Edmunds, Suffolk IP33 2AQ, or St Andrews House, 41 West Nile St, Glasgow G1 2RU in Scotland. An application may be made to the appropriate ROET. The ROET are based in Bedford, Birmingham, Bristol, Bury St Edmunds, Cardiff, Leeds, London (Central, East and South), Manchester, Newcastle upon Tyne, Nottingham and Southampton. For addresses, see Chapter 12.

Ensure that the application is presented in time. The main time limits on termination of employment are (subject to exceptional cases):

(a) unfair dismissal – before the effective date of termination or within three months from the effective date of termination except in the (unusual) case of unfair selection of strikers for re-engagement after industrial action when the applicant has six months from the applicant's date of dismissal;

(b) reasons for dismissal – within three months from the effective date of termination: ERA, s 93(3);

(c) race discrimination – within three months from the date of the act complained of: Race Relations Act 1976, s 68(1)(6);

(d) redundancy payments – within six months of the relevant date of termination: ERA, s 164(1);

(e) sex and race discrimination – three months from the date of the act complained of, save in the case of complaints of instructions to discriminate, persistent discrimination and pressure to discriminate, in which cases six months (in these cases, only the EOC and CRE may bring complaints): Sex Discrimination Act 1975, s 76(2) and (4).

For complete list see Chapter 10.

4.2.2 Date of presentation

In most cases of unfair dismissal, the application must be presented within three months from the effective date of termination, that is:

(a) where the dismissal is with notice, the date when the notice expires;

(b) where the dismissal is without notice, the date when the termination takes effect;

(c) where the contract is for a fixed term, the date when the fixed term expires.

A claim for unfair dismissal may be brought during the period of notice, that is, before the effective date of termination.

4.2.3 Extending the time limit

In the case of remedies for unfair dismissal and failure to give written reasons for dismissal, the time limit may be extended for such further period as the employment tribunal considers reasonable in a case where it is satisfied it was not reasonably practicable for the application to be presented before the end of the period of three months. The period may be extended for discrimination and redundancy payment applications if the tribunal considers it just and equitable to do so, which gives the tribunal a wider discretion than in unfair dismissal cases. The question to be asked in unfair dismissal applications is whether it is feasible to present the claim within the period. If an applicant is advised by a lawyer or other skilled advisor, it is unlikely to be determined that it was not practicable for him to claim within the time limits but each case depends on its facts (*Ryback v Jean Sorrelle Ltd* [1991] ICR 127; *London International College v Sen* [1992] IRCR 292).

Time is also unlikely to be extended on the grounds that:

(a) domestic appeal hearings are taking place,

(b) settlement talks are going on, or

(c) criminal proceedings are being heard,

but likely excuses which may be acceptable include physical impediment, absence abroad or a postal strike.

The question of the seriousness of a period of disabling illness varies depending on whether it occurred in the earlier weeks or the more critical weeks leading up to the expiry of the limitation period (*Schultz v Esso Petroleum Ltd* [1999] ICR 1202). On domestic appeals and the time limit in discrimination cases, see *Aniagwu v London Borough of Hackney* [1999] IRLR 303. For full discussion of effective date of termination, relevant date of termination and date of dismissal (three separate concepts) and on discretionary extension of those time limits, see Bowers, J, *Bowers on Employment Law*, 5th edn, 2000.

4.2.4 Rules about presentation

(a) The application is presented when it is received by the tribunal, whether or not it is dealt with by the tribunal staff immediately on receipt.

(b) On a weekend or Bank Holiday an application may be presented by posting it through the letter box of the ROET or COET.

(c) Don't leave things to the last minute. If there may be a problem about complying with a time limit and the application is sent by post, it is the representative's duty to ensure that it has arrived safely and the representative may be liable to the applicant if he fails in his duty.

The posting rules: s 7 of the Interpretation Act 1978 applies to posting letters to and by the employment tribunal. This means that where service is effected by ordinary post, service is deemed to be effected by properly addressing, prepaying and posting a letter, and unless and until the contrary is proved, the letter will be treated as delivered in the ordinary course of post, that is, assumed to be two days for first class mail and four days for second class mail.

4.2.5 Refusal to register the application

If the Secretary of Tribunals believes that the applicant is not entitled to seek the relief requested in the Originating Application (because of, for example, inadequate continuity of service, see 2.1 above) or that it is outside the jurisdiction of the employment tribunal (for example, because it makes a contractual claim which is not within Pt II of the ERA 1996 or arising on termination of employment), he may notify the applicant of this belief, and state that the application will not be registered unless and until the applicant states in writing that he wishes to proceed. If the applicant desires to go ahead, the matter will probably be determined at a preliminary hearing.

4.2.6 Special applicants and respondents

A company in liquidation

In the case of a company which has been wound up by order of the court or where a provisional liquidator has been appointed, employment tribunal proceedings may be commenced or pursued only by leave of the Companies Court (Companies Act 1985, s 525(2); see *Carr v British International Helicopters Ltd* [1994] ICR 18).

An overseas company

The main employment legislation applies to any activities in British Territorial Waters; activities connected with the exploration of a sea bed, sub-soil or the exploration of their natural resources, and any activities connected with exploration or exploitation of the Frigg Gas Field.

The President or regional chairman has a discretion to allow service out of the UK in any case where there is no address for service within the jurisdiction.

A deceased employer or employee

If there is no appointed personal representative of a deceased employee, employment tribunal proceedings may be instituted or continued on behalf of the employee by such other person as the employment tribunal appoints to pursue them. An application is made to this effect to the employment tribunal, and is either the person authorised by the employee to so act before he died, or the widower, widow, child, father, mother, brother or sister of the deceased. Any award will be made in favour of the estate of the deceased (ERA, ss 206 and 207). A cause of action in discrimination does not die with the applicant: *Harris v Lewisham and Guys Mental Health Trust* [2000] IRLR 320.

Substituted service

If the applicant does not know the respondent's address, the tribunal may make an order for substituted service, usually by an advertisement in a local newspaper, where it circulates in the area where the party is thought to reside or carry on business. This is very rarely done.

4.2.7 Service of Form IT1

The appropriate ROET serves the Originating Application on the respondent named in it initially by first or second class post together with a standard form printed Notice of Appearance (IT3) for the defence of the respondent (see Chapter 9). The ROET also sends an accompanying, explanatory notice (Standard Form IT2) which indicates the case number allotted to the application and outlines the procedure. This case number should be quoted in all later correspondence with the ROET about the case.

Service of these documents is generally deemed to be effective at the time at which the letter is delivered in the ordinary course of the post. If it has not been received, the ROET sends another copy by recorded delivery.

4.2.8 Submitting the notice of appearance

The respondent's defence is called the Notice of Appearance, and should be submitted to the ROET within 21 days of receipt of the Originating Application. The official form (IT3) does not have to be used but it is sensible to do so. (See Chapter 9.)

4.2.9 Defaulting respondent

If a respondent has not presented a notice of appearance within the allotted time of 21 days, he cannot take part in the proceedings brought by the applicant save that he may ask for extra time to submit his claim or apply for a review (see 6.5 below) on the ground that he received no notice of the application. He may also appear as a witness and be sent a copy of the employment tribunal's decision.

5 Conciliation and Preparation

5.1 ACAS Conciliation Officer

The Regional Office of Employment Tribunals (ROET) sends a copy of every originating application to an employment tribunal in its area (save those which claim only redundancy payments) to an Advisory Conciliation and Arbitration Service (ACAS) Conciliation Officer who may telephone you about the case or even suggest a round table meeting. The degree of active involvement varies between officers.

Note:

(a) Discussions with the conciliation officer are confidential, and may not be referred to at the hearing.

(b) The conciliation officer has no duty to inform the parties of the relevant legislation and has no duty to act as an advisor to any party.

(c) An agreement reached through the conciliation officer's good offices need not be in writing to be effective.

(d) ACAS are not prepared merely to sign a COT3 and will not, become involved before an application to the employment tribunal has been lodged.

5.2 Settlement

If you have settled, ensure that the settlement is recorded on ACAS Form COT3 or a valid compromise agreement. A claim may be settled at various stages:

(a) before an originating application has been presented (although the ACAS conciliation officer will not intervene unless the employee has been dismissed or has resigned and the prospective applicant could bring a claim and would have done so if he had not intervened);

(b) between the originating application and the hearing;

(c) on the day of the hearing or during the hearing.

In the first two cases (and especially if you are acting for the respondent), ensure that the agreement is clearly recorded by the ACAS Conciliation Officer. If the Conciliation Officer has not 'taken action' in relation to the agreement, it cannot restrict the right of the employee to bring another claim. 'Taking action' may involve nothing more onerous than recording the terms of settlement. This will be best achieved on the official Form COT3. The usual formula on that form is:

> The respondent will pay to the applicant the sum of £x in full and final settlement of these proceedings and of all other (if any) claims which the applicant may have against the respondent arising out of the terms and conditions of his contract of employment or out of its termination.

A compromise agreement is valid to settle a claim to an employment tribunal if it is in writing, the employee has received independent legal advice from a qualified lawyer or relevant independent adviser which may include a trade union official, employee or certified member of a trade union; or, a certified employee or volunteer working at an advice centre; or, a person specified by the Secretary of State and the adviser is covered by an insurance policy. See *Lunt v Merseyside TEC Ltd* [1999] ICR 17.

5.3 Consent order

When an agreement settling the case is reported to it, the employment tribunal usually draws up an order that all further proceedings be stayed save insofar as it may be necessary to carry the agreed terms into effect and contains a schedule setting out the agreed terms. The schedule is not in itself part of the order of the tribunal. Alternatively, it may dismiss the application on withdrawal by the applicant.

If the case is settled at the tribunal itself, the tribunal will normally have the agreement drawn up as a Consent Order made by the tribunal to dispose of the application. Frequently, the applicant will undertake to withdraw his application only at such time as the respondent pays the agreed sum. Practice does differ between different regions, and different employment tribunal chairmen. The tribunals have different preferences, and have various standard forms for recording settlements. If it provides for a payment of money, the order will be enforceable in the county court in the same way as the order of an employment tribunal (see 6.6 below). The settlement may well be more wide ranging than this and contain provisions for confidentiality, provision of a reference, an apology, return of documents or a car or the like. If disobeyed, these would have to be enforced by separate action on the contract in the High Court or county court and not by the employment tribunal, which has no jurisdiction to enforce contracts or its own orders.

Any settlement may be enforced as an ordinary contract, and can be set aside on the same grounds as a contract, such as mistake or (very rarely) duress.

5.4   Interlocutory applications

5.4.1 Striking out

The whole or part of an originating application or notice of appearance may be struck out on the grounds that:

(a) it is scandalous, that is, it raises matters not fit to be raised in an employment tribunal;

(b) it is frivolous, that is, it is so manifestly misconceived as to have no prospect of success;

(c) it is vexatious, that is the claim has been presented without any expectation of success, but out of spite or to harass the respondent;

(d) the party fails to comply with an order made by the employment tribunal for further and better particulars, answers to written questions or discovery (see 5.4.3 and 5.4.4 below);

(e) for want of prosecution, but employment tribunals very rarely strike out on this ground.

The employment tribunals are used to dealing with 'homemade pleadings' and unrepresented parties and only very rarely exercise the power to strike out. A party whose Originating Application or Notice of Appearance may be struck out must be given an opportunity to be heard as to why such an order should not be made against him.

5.4.2 Amendments

The applicant or respondent may amend the application and notice of appearance respectively at any time with the leave of the employment tribunal.

Note

(a) The employment tribunal may allow a new cause of action to be added outside the time limit (for example, *BNPC v Kelly* [1989] ICR 221), but recently a more restrictive approach has been taken (*Selkent Bus Co Ltd v Moore* [1996] ICR 836; *Harvey v Port of Tilbury (London) Ltd* [1999] ICR 1030), cf *Gillick v BP Chemicals* [1993] IRLR 437.

(b) Leave to amend is dispensed liberally, provided that the other party is not prejudiced by the amendment and it will not usually be prejudiced if the application is made in good time before the tribunal hearing.

(c) The name of the respondent is often amended and this may occur even after the hearing of the claim.

5.4.3 Further and Better Particulars

The employment tribunal has power to order either party to give Further and Better Particulars of its case and contentions.

Application

The party requesting such details should first write to the other side seeking this information by a particular date and only if that person refuses them or delays replying should an application for an order be addressed to the employment tribunal. Such application should be made in good time before the hearing.

Will the request be granted?

Practice differs between different chairmen and depending on the inherent complexity of the case, but generally employment tribunals are reluctant to sanction very extensive requests. In one case, the Employment Appeal Tribunal (EAT) said that 'in one way or another the parties need to know the sort of thing which is going to be the subject of the hearing' (*White v University of Manchester* [1976] ICR 419). This is particularly important in probing the employer's case on the reasons for dismissal. He should not be allowed merely to claim that, for example, the employee was 'incompetent and incapable' but asked to give all facts on which he will rely for this contention.

Disobedience to an order

If a party disobeys an order by the employment tribunal for further and better particulars, his 'pleading' or part of it may be struck out. If there is a possibility of such a strike out, the employment tribunal must give the party at risk an opportunity to show cause why such an order should not be made against him.

Questionnaire procedure

In race, sex and disability discrimination cases, the applicant may deliver to the respondent a special questionnaire which goes further than a request for further and better particulars and probes the evidence which is to be given at the tribunal. A standard outline form questionnaire is available from the Commission for Racial Equality, Equal Opportunities Commission and Disability Rights Commission respectively (for addresses, see Chapter 12). The employment tribunal has no power to compel a party to answer this questionnaire but the replies are admissible as evidence before the employment tribunal and if the employer omits to reply within a reasonable time or is evasive or equivocal in the replies he gives, the employment tribunal may infer, if it considers it just and equitable to do so, that such failure or refusal may be evidence that the employer has committed the unlawful act alleged against him (s 74 of the Sex Discrimination Act 1975, s 65(2)(b) of the Race Relations Act 1976, s 56 of the Disability Discrimination Act 1995).

5.4.4 Discovery of documents

The employment tribunal has the same powers in respect of discovery and inspection as does the county court. Discovery means indicating what documents are in the possession, custody or control of the party, while inspection involves permitting the other party to look at those documents. In practice, most representatives will supply (usually at the cost of the other party) photocopies of those documents which his opponent(s) want to see. There is no automatic disclosure of all relevant documents and no formal lists are exchanged as in the civil courts. Rather, the employment tribunal only should order such disclosure as is necessary in order to dispose fairly of the proceedings or to save costs. This gives the employment tribunal chairman a general discretion to determine what should be discovered. In general:

(a) Confidential personnel reports and other confidential documents (such as medical reports) should only be disclosed if they are necessary for disposing fairly of the proceedings. In many cases, the employment tribunal chairman will consider the documents himself before deciding whether they should be disclosed (see *Nasse v Science Research Council* [1980] AC 1028).

(b) There is unlikely to be an order for discovery of documents which merely go to the credibility of a witness.

(c) It may be appropriate to order discovery of documents relating to another employee if the applicant claims that the manner in which he has been treated is inconsistent with the treatment given to a fellow employee.

(d) Disclosure of documents relating to compensation will not normally be ordered until liability has been determined.

(e) Disclosure will not be ordered when it would be 'oppressive' to do so. In one case, a request for discovery would have meant that some 600,000 documents would have had to be disclosed. The Court of Appeal decided that a representative sample only need be given to the other side.

Although there is no automatic discovery rule in employment tribunals as in the High Court, it is important that advisors do not mislead the tribunal by making selective disclosure of documents. This was emphasised by Waite P in *Birds Eye Ltd v Harrison* [1985] IRLR 48 when he said:

> ... any party who chooses to make voluntary disclosure of any documents in his possession or power must not be unfairly selective in his disclosure ... it becomes his duty not to withhold from discovery any further documents in his possession or power (regardless of whether they support his case or not) if there is any risk that the effect of withholding them might be to convey to his opponent or to the employment tribunal a false or misleading impression as to the true nature, purport or effect of any disclosed document.

A party who wishes to see documents in the possession of the other should write a letter giving the other party a time limit for compliance. If there is no or insufficient response to this request, an application should be made to the tribunal in the form of a letter. If a document is in the possession of a third party, the tribunal can order him to attend the hearing and produce the document.

5.4.5 Witness orders

Any party may apply to the employment tribunal for a witness order against a person in Great Britain (Employment Tribunal Rules, r 4(2)). The order should only be granted if it is necessary. Indeed, it is not sensible to obtain a witness order on a hostile witness as you cannot cross-examine one of your own witnesses. Letters relating to a witness order, unlike correspondence on other interlocutory matters are not copied by the ROET to the other party.

Note

(a) A party has no obligation to inform the other as to the witnesses it intends to call at the hearing, but it may be wise to do so if one wishes to know the other side's position.

(b) A witness who fails to attend when an order is made against him may be fined up to Level 3 on the standard scale (Employment Tribunals Act 1996, s 7(4)).

(c) It is desirable to agree to exchange witness statements say about seven days before the hearing because: (1) it helps to decide whether it would be best to do a deal as you can weigh up your evidence and that of the other side; (2) it helps the advocate to prepare his or her cross-examination; (3) references in witness statements to pages in the agreed bundle can be inserted into witness statements.

(d) The witness statement should deal with the material facts, be set out chronologically in numbered paragraphs and be written in the witness' own words rather than in the manner of a pleading.

5.4.6 Interlocutory applications

The employment tribunal may at any stage give directions on any matter in connection with proceedings before it. Such applications are usually made by letter to the Secretary of Tribunals or regional secretary, and in most cases dealt with by a tribunal chairman alone without an oral hearing. In the case of controversial issues, a hearing may be arranged for all parties to attend to present oral arguments. No special forms are required in making an application for an interlocutory hearing. You should make clear in your letter to the ROET precisely the point on which you want the employment tribunal to adjudicate and your arguments in support.

5.4.7 Joining parties to the proceedings

An employment tribunal has power under the Employment Tribunal Rules to join as a respondent a party against whom any relief is sought or to dismiss a respondent who does not appear to be directly interested in the subject matter of the application. An employment tribunal must make such an order in a case where before the hearing there is an application for a person or trade union to be joined so that compensation can be awarded against such person or trade union because he or it put pressure on the employer to secure the dismissal (Trade Union and Labour Relations (Consolidation) Act 1992, s 150).

5.4.8 Combination of applications

The employment tribunal may combine two or more pending applications where:

(a) some common question of law or fact arises in both or all the applications; or

(b) the relief claimed arises out of the same set of facts; or

(c) for some other reason it is desirable to make such an order.

There may be important tactical considerations in proposing or opposing combination. The parties concerned must be given the opportunity to show cause why such an order should not be made. Where two or more cases are heard together, the employment tribunal must still separately consider the facts of each. In mass redundancy or strike dismissal cases, it may be convenient to treat one or more cases as 'test' or 'sample' cases. There were about 4,500 unfair dismissal cases arising out of the Wapping dispute between News International and the printing unions in 1986 and they were to be heard together but all save two settled without a hearing!

5.4.9 Pre-hearing review

A respondent may ask for a pre-hearing review of the applicant's case. In theory the applicant can ask for a pre-hearing review of his own case or of the respondent's contentions but this rarely happens in practice. The employment tribunal does not have to agree to hold a pre-hearing review and will refuse to do so where the claim inevitably raises contested issues of fact which only oral evidence may resolve. Indeed some regions do not hold pre-hearing reviews as a matter of practice. The employment tribunal may call a pre-hearing review of its own accord if it considers the contentions of the party to be weak. At such a hearing, the tribunal may order a party to deposit up to £150 'as a condition of being permitted to continue to take part in the proceedings relating to that matter' (Employment Tribunal Rules, r 7(4)). If, at the full hearing, an order of costs is made against that party who has been ordered to pay a deposit the deposit is forfeit (r 12(8)).

5.5 Preparing for the hearing

5.5.1 Notice of hearing

The employment tribunal should give at least 14 days' notice to the parties of the date of hearing. The letter setting the date also gives basic procedural information. The ROET at which the hearing will take place will normally make contact with the parties some time before issuing the notice of hearing to discover whether the date is convenient for the parties and/or their representatives and/or witnesses. Shorter notice is valid only with the consent of both (or all) the parties. Some employment tribunal offices list for a hearing for directions for every discrimination case.

5.5.2 Length of hearing

Indicate to the ROET if you think that a case will take longer than a day. The ROET will ask the parties for this time estimate before listing the case, but some will not on principle list cases for more than one or two days whatever the complexity and length of the case as assessed by the parties. This is because it may be difficult to secure the continuous attendance of the lay members (most of whom have regular employment) over longer periods. If the case overruns its allotted time it is unlikely (in most tribunals) to be continued on the following days since other cases will have been fixed for those subsequent days. Depending on the commitments of the tribunal members, the representatives and witnesses, the case may have to be adjourned for long periods, sometimes three months or more. This is highly frustrating and unsatisfactory and should encourage parties to give a realistic time estimate from the start. It is important to co-operate fully with the Listing Office of the Tribunal.

5.5.3 Bundle of documents

Well before the hearing date, the parties should consider whether they can agree a bundle of documents to go before the employment tribunal. The fact that a party agrees that a particular document should go into the bundle does not mean that the party necessarily agrees with its contents, or to the use to which the other party may put the document, merely that it may be referred to in the tribunal hearing. In most cases, this may occur by means of a photocopy. It is advisable to send a bundle to the tribunal in good time before the hearing, although not all tribunals will actually read the bundle before the hearing. Indeed, you may find that you are 'switched' at the last moment to a different tribunal from that before which you were due to appear. In that case, they will not have had an opportunity to read anything but the 'pleadings'. Much time may be wasted in a tribunal hearing if the bundle is not properly put together and numbered beforehand and the party that fails to do so will soon lose the sympathy of the tribunal. The following hints should be borne in mind.

(a) Ensure that the bundle is in a logical order. Normally, a chronological order will be most appropriate but, where there are several issues in a case, it may be more suitable to arrange the documents around those issues. For example, a hearing may have to consider in a case of alleged unfair dismissal in a redundancy case:

- whether there was a redundancy;
- whether the employer behaved reasonably in all the circumstances in relation to consultation, and in considering suitable alternative employment;
- compensation.

It may be most helpful in such a case to divide the documentation into three separate bundles or three separate dividers of a loose-leaf folder. Again, it is frequently appropriate to put solicitors' correspondence in a separate divider or bundle. Parties should provide three bundles for the tribunal (of three members), one for a witness and at least one for the use of each party, that is, six as minimum.

(b) Number each page consecutively; this is easier to understand and follow than numbering each document consecutively. These practical suggestions are made as to numbering:

- that every page must have a unique number, late inserts can be numbered 41a, 41b, etc;
- the page numbers should be written in black ink;
- the numbers should be in the bottom right hand corner (easier to see when flicking through the bundle), possibly in a circle and located on the page in a position where they will not be omitted during photocopying;
- the numbers must be big enough to see;
- the bundles should always be in a lever arch file with room for further documents to be inserted if necessary during the hearing.

(c) In a highly complex case with hundreds of pages of documents, it may be appropriate to have a 'core bundle' of the most important documents in order to lessen the need to leaf through to, say, page 187 to find it; you can also ask the employment tribunal to read at least this bundle before the employment tribunal starts.

(d) Prepare an outline chronology, a list of issues and dramatis personae to assist the tribunal.

(e) Only refuse to agree a bundle with your opponent if there is some vital reason for objecting to the admissibility of a particular document, for example, on grounds of privilege. A party which needlessly causes the employment tribunal to have two rival bundles or duplicate documents within a single bundle is unlikely to find favour with the employment tribunal. If (which would be rare) there may be a dispute about the admissibility or authenticity of various documents, they should be hived off into a separate applicant or respondent bundle.

(f) Do not refuse to agree a bundle in the hope of taking your opponent by surprise since a party doing so may have to pay the costs of any adjournment necessitated thereby.

(g) It may be possible to go beyond an agreed bundle to agreeing a statement of the uncontroversial facts with your opponents, so that time is not wasted on them in the hearing. Alternatively, witness statements may be exchanged as is now the practice in the High Court and the county court. Some tribunals insist on such an exchange or at least that such statements are produced at the hearing as 'evidence in chief'.

(h) Ensure that all copies are legible and show a complete page.

5.5.4 Postponing a hearing

The employment tribunal may postpone a hearing and the EAT will not interfere with its decision to do so or to refuse an adjournment unless it is perverse. You may want a postponement because:

(a) other proceedings relating to the same facts are pending in the civil or criminal courts, but this fact is not always decisive;

(b) a representative is unavailable;

(c) an important witness cannot attend: an employment tribunal is likely to probe the reasons for the inability to attend and (especially where a party initially indicated that the date or dates were suitable) to be sympathetic to an adjournment only if it is a genuinely important pre-arranged fixture or unexpected ill health.

Tribunals will not permit the parties (especially the employer in whose interest it may be to postpone the proceedings) to indulge in time-wasting activities in order to gain a perceived tactical advantage.

5.5.5 Hearings in private

Employment tribunals are normally open to the public but may sit in camera for all or some part of a case where the evidence or part of the evidence:

(a) involves matters of national security;

(b) would result in disclosures contrary to statutory provisions;

(c) consists of information communicated in confidence;

(d) would involve substantial injury to the employer's undertaking other than any effects it might have on collective bargaining.

Such private hearings are very rare. On other occasions, an employment tribunal may restrict the use of a person's name in order to preserve anonymity (say of a mentally ill patient, a sexually harassed applicant or an unsuccessful applicant for a post).

Further, the employment tribunal may make a restricted reporting order prohibiting the naming of individuals concerned in allegations of sexual misconduct but only until the promulgation of the employment tribunal decision. This extends to sexual harassment and 'other adverse conduct of whatever nature related to sex' and 'the sexual orientation of the person at whom the conduct is directed', but this cannot be made in favour of a company (*Leicester University v A* [1999] ICR 701; see, also, *A v B ex p News Group*

Newspapers Ltd [1998] ICR 55). A restricted reporting order can also be used in a disability case where there is evidence of a personal nature meaning 'any evidence of a medical, or other intimate, nature which might reasonably be assumed to be likely to cause significant embarrassment to the complainant if reported' (ss 11 and 12 of the Employment Tribunals Act 1996).

5.5.6 Representations in writing

The parties may submit written representations to the employment tribunal but must send them in not less than seven days before the hearing. A party should only rely on this procedure in exceptional circumstances since a written statement is bound to have less force than evidence given in the tribunal room, where the tribunal members can consider the manner in which the evidence is given and hear it being tested in cross-examination.

5.5.7 Absence of a party

If an applicant or respondent fails to attend the hearing, the employment tribunal may:

(a) dismiss the applicant's case or respondent's defence as the case may be;

(b) hear the application in his absence;

(c) adjourn the hearing to another date.

In practice, the tribunal clerk will telephone the missing party and give him time to attend. The employment tribunal must bear in mind the fact that if the party has a good reason for his absence, he may later apply for a review (see 6.5). An employment tribunal should consider the IT1, IT3 and any written representations/answers before dismissing or disposing of any application (1993 Regulations, r 9(3)).

5.5.8 Preparation

(a) Determine which witnesses are necessary and desirable – seek to avoid:

- applying for witness orders because witnesses who have to be forced to attend may turn out to be hostile or merely unhelpful or suffering from amnesia;
- calling too many witnesses who may contradict each other.

Remember that hearsay (whilst undesirable, if avoidable) is permissible in tribunals but should be kept to moderate quantities.

(b) Anticipate the questions your opponent is likely to ask of your witnesses and ensure that you have covered these points in your statements.

(c) Reassess the strength and weaknesses of the opposing party in the light of the results of any interlocutory 'skirmishes': has the process of discovery thrown up any surprises? need further witness statements be taken?

(d) Check whether the hearing is to cover liability only, liability and contributory fault, liability and remedy, or some other combination of issues.

6 The Hearing

6.1 Arriving at the hearing

(a) Seek out the tribunal clerk who will need to take a note of parties, representatives, witnesses (with their positions) and observers and discover the Department of Social Security office from which an applicant may have received benefit since his dismissal.

(b) You should also at this stage hand in to the clerk a list of cases on which you may wish to rely. Most tribunal centres have copies of the Industrial Relations Law Reports, Industrial Cases Reports and Industrial Tribunal Reports (now discontinued), but most representatives now prefer the parties to produce photocopies of relevant authorities. Most do not have copies of the standard law reports, so that if you need to refer to such a report, it is essential to take a photocopy with you. You need to bring a copy of each authority for each member of the tribunal and one for the other party, that is, four copies. Do not cite too many cases. The tribunals have copies of the relevant individual employment law statutes but usually no other legislation. Most tribunals are fully familiar with the leading cases, and will not appreciate advocates reading them out unnecessarily.

(c) Enquire whether the tribunal has seen and read any documents sent in in advance.

(d) Check what time the case will actually start. Although listed to start at 10am, you may find on arrival that your case is a 'floater' and will be taken by the first tribunal to become available (for example, after hearing a short interlocutory application, or after there has been a settlement in another case).

(e) If you have not appeared before the particular tribunal before, ask the clerk for useful information about the manner in which the chairman 'runs' the tribunal; For example, the degree of formality adopted; whether (s)he frowns on opening speeches; whether he is slow or 'brisk' in conducting the proceedings and his attitude to the citation of authorities. This is especially sound advice.

(f) Ask for expense forms relating to travel and loss of wages for the witnesses.

(g) Gain some guidance on when the employment tribunal is likely to rise for lunch (usually between 12.30pm and 1.30pm, or 1pm and 2pm) and finish its session in the afternoon, usually 4pm or 4.30pm.

Most tribunal clerks are very helpful and friendly. With the permission of the tribunal chairman, the clerk may be prepared to carry out some small amount of photocopying required for late arrived documents but do not overreach his or her goodwill in this respect.

Explain to each witness the procedure to be adopted by the employment tribunal, and:

(a) give him pen and paper so that he can inform you of his comments on the other evidence and stress that he should give you the details as they occur to him, since it may be too late at the next adjournment. It is much less distracting to be handed a note than to have words muttered in your ear when you are seeking to listen to the witnesses and/or the members of the employment tribunal (and there is also a risk that the employment tribunal members may overhear what is being said; many have finely tuned antennae!);

(b) ask whether he wishes to take an oath or to affirm;

(c) run through his evidence without 'coaching' or 'briefing' him;

(d) tell him not to speak to the press before he has given his evidence and to be careful of any comments he makes afterwards;

(e) tell him to speak slowly and clearly since the tribunal chairman will make a handwritten note of all the evidence;

(f) tell him that if he genuinely does not understand a question he should ask for it to be clarified and not just blunder on.

Don't be afraid to ask for a short adjournment to clarify an issue with a witness (although, obviously not when the witness is giving evidence). This often saves time in the long run, and if you don't 'get it straight' before the end of cross-examination, it may be too late. Some employment tribunals regularly rise mid-way through the morning and afternoon sessions for a 5–10 minutes' break.

Normally, the applicant and his party sit on the right hand side facing the tribunal and the respondent sits on the left side.

6.2 Presenting a case

There is an old adage that 90% of cases are not affected by advocacy: 5% are lost by bad advocacy, 3% are won by good advocacy and 2% are totally wild. This section, thus, contains as much psychology as law and practice. As an advocate, you should think of yourself as the honest guide of the employment tribunal, forceful but fair, helping them on their way through the journey of the case. Remember that your main aim is to convince the three tribunal members of the justness of your case, and that this process will not be assisted or achieved by theatrical displays, heavy handed questioning, or attacks on the senses, patience or nerves of the tribunal itself. Be careful not to bore the tribunal! There are no hard and fast rules appropriate to all cases, but the following general principles should assist.

6.2.1 Opening speech

Most tribunals do not want a long, or indeed any, opening speech (and indeed there is no 'right' to make such a speech in the Employment Tribunal Rules). A chairman may make clear his displeasure with a representative merely telling the employment tribunal what he hopes his witnesses will say in evidence to the tribunal, especially since those witnesses will be sitting in the room listening! An opening may, however, be appropriate when the facts are complex and will require several witnesses to unfold them or where the documents are voluminous, or where there are difficult legal issues.

The evidence before the employment tribunal begins with the party on whom the burden of proof rests and these rules apply.

(a) If the fact of dismissal is disputed by the respondent who says, for example, that the applicant resigned or there was a mutually agreed termination of employment, then the applicant usually goes first as the tribunal will have to find if there has been a dismissal. This will particularly apply in complaints of constructive dismissal. If there is no dismissal then that ends the applicant's case.

(b) Except where there is a dispute about dismissal, the applicant begins since he must satisfy the tribunal that he has been dismissed.

(c) The respondent must prove the reason for dismissal so that he would open the case where dismissal is admitted.

(d) There is no onus of proof on the employer to prove that he behaved reasonably in all the circumstances of a dismissal, but the normal practice in employment tribunals is that the employer opens on this issue even if the reason for dismissal is admitted. He is usually best placed to set the scene for the evidence which follows, and is likely to be more familiar with the documentation.

(e) In discrimination cases, the applicant opens.

If there are mixed complaints, that is, unfair dismissal and that the dismissal was an act of racial discrimination, and there is no agreement as to who is to go first then speak to your opponent and see whether you can both put a common proposition to the tribunal as to who goes first. In any event they may not agree with you.

First, ask the tribunal whether the members have read the papers. All members of the employment tribunal will almost certainly have seen the Originating Application, Notice of Appearance and any other 'pleadings'. It may be appropriate to then go through the bundle, and you should ensure that it is in a logical order. Ask the employment tribunal whether they would prefer as a general practice to read the documents for themselves or that you should read them aloud to them. As a general rule do not make an opening speech if only one witness will give evidence and, increasingly, tribunals do not want opening speeches at all. It may be helpful at this stage to identify points the employment tribunal will have to decide, although it is neither necessary nor probably desirable to give a full legal exposition of them. Citation of cases should await the closing speech. Check whether the employment tribunal will be dealing with liability first, then compensation, or with the two issues together. It may be helpful to present an outline chronology, a list of *dramatis personae* and a note of the legal and factual issues which are likely to arise. Show these to your opponent in advance of the case to ensure that he does not object to any part of them going before the tribunal. It is a matter of common courtesy to seek out the other side. What do you do if he or she is unrepresented? It is good sense to talk to the other party about the nature and structure of the tribunal hearing and also to explain what propositions your case law authorities are for.

Secondly, if your witness intends to swear an oath, then find out upon which holy book and then inform the tribunal clerk so that he or she can provide a copy.

6.2.2 Questioning

(a) Don't be monotonous and, above all, do not bore the tribunal.

(b) There will be occasions when witnesses (including your own) do not give the evidence you expected. Although it may be obvious to them that this has happened from the tenor of your question and the nature of answer given to it, do not indicate your surprise to the witness or the tribunal (for example, by an open mouth). If you are completely 'thrown' by a piece of evidence (which will be unusual), you can ask for a short adjournment, although there is no guarantee that you will get it.

(c) Watch the chairman's pen, since he has to take a note of all the proceedings and cannot write as fast as many witnesses speak. Advise your witnesses to watch that pen and when answering your questions to address the employment tribunal – not the questioner.

(d) Never seem at a loss for words: make it appear you have a continuous course of questions prepared; don't fumble around for papers.

(e) Don't interrupt the replies by a witness to your questions even if (frustratingly) the answer does not connect directly with those questions.

(f) Remember that some witnesses (for example, doctors, police officers) may be very familiar with being examined and court practice whilst others will never have appeared in a court or tribunal before.

(g) Be self-confident without being over-confident.

(h) If you are faced by a chairman who constantly interrupts your questions, be polite but firm and ensure that you ask all the questions you need to ask.

(i) Keep up the momentum of your questioning; don't flag.

(j) Remember to warn your witnesses that they may not discuss the case whilst they are in the course of giving evidence.

(k) Remember that the tribunal will be able to see (and possibly hear!) what is going on at the back of the tribunal room, so it is important that witnesses do not gesticulate or speak about the evidence being given.

6.2.3 Examination in chief

(a) Do not ask leading questions: ask 'When is your birthday?' not 'Is your birthday 1 January?': although time can be saved before the employment tribunal by asking leading questions on uncontroversial matters such as the date of commencement of employment, the nature of the employer's business, the work history, etc (but note that each issue may be highly contentious in particular cases). Ask your opponent and the tribunal whether they object to your 'leading' on such matters.

(b) Don't give evidence yourself.

(c) Think carefully about the order in which your witnesses should be called: in most cases, there will be one 'lead' witness, for example, the applicant himself, or the dismissing officer; usually the 'lead witness' should be called first (and the tribunal may raise their eyebrows if the applicant is not called first for his side). In many cases, it will be appropriate to have the evidence build up in a chronological sequence, but in other cases it will be more logical if it proceeds issue by issue. Assess carefully in advance the strength and weakness of each witness to be called. Where you have several witnesses, it may be helpful to place a 'good' witness at the start and at the end of the sequence.

(d) When you have completed your questioning, make sure that you have got the whole story out; check any statement from the witness carefully at the end; most employment tribunal chairmen are sympathetic to the difficulties and will give you a few minutes to check this. Remember that you will not get a second chance. In most cases, witnesses will be 'released' from further attendance at the employment tribunal after they have given evidence.

(e) Do not be afraid to bring out your weak points: it is better that they first come out in evidence in chief if they are bound to arise in any case.

6.2.4 Cross-examination

Most people view cross-examination as the most difficult of the arts or skills of examination. If this is of any comfort, remember that no one (not even the most skilled QC) knows at the start of the cross-examination how he will come out at the end of it, and that the witness will probably be more frightened than you are. Cross-examination is always a risky process. Many people advise never to ask a question you don't know the answer to, but this is probably unrealistic advice to follow. The following principles may help, but only experience can master the art.

(a) Have in mind clear aims in your questioning of the particular witness. Your task is to elicit evidence, not to comment as you go along. A great legal point may well occur to you in the middle of the cross-examination, but don't blurt it out, as it may not occur to your opponent and you should not give him time to research it well before his closing speech (when he would otherwise hear of it possibly for the first time).

(b) You essentially have a two-fold aim in your questioning, to weaken the case for the other side and to establish facts favourable to your own. In doing this, it is commonly said that there are four techniques: confrontation, undermining, insinuation, and probing. Plan which feature (or combination of features) you are going to adopt in any series of questions, and follow that plan.

(c) Don't feel you have not 'earned your fee' if you don't carry out an interminable cross-examination – often the shorter the better. Sometimes you may not need to cross-examine at all. Do not get emotionally involved in the case and do not let this shine through in your cross-examination.

(d) Keep your questions short: as a general rule, each one should occupy no more than one line of transcript.

(e) Ask only one question at a time and have a clear aim for each question.

(f) Be precise in the questions you ask: don't let the witness score a point by asking you *which* question he should answer.

(g) Do not be tempted to give evidence yourself.

(h) Keep a list of topics to cover and keep a list of outline questions. Everyone has a different approach to this, but it is probably unwise to prepare questions in too great detail before the hearing, since you do not know precisely what evidence will be given and how it will be given and it will be the more difficult to adjust your approach later.

(i) If there has been an exchange of witness statements, then this may provide the opportunity to prepare detailed cross-examination as you will know what the other party's witnesses are going to say.

(j) You may succeed in casting doubt on the credibility of the other side by probing relentlessly some apparently insignificant or peripheral aspect of the case.

(k) Assess your objectives with each witness. You will probably not need to discredit *every* witness for your opponent; sometimes, you may wish to describe a witness called by your opponent as fair and accurate in the summing up: nothing will be served by a general attack on his or her credibility.

(l) End the cross-examination on a high note.

(m) Always be civil to the witness; do not raise your voice; you don't want the employment tribunal to think, 'Thank God, he is not cross-examining me!' The lay members of the employment tribunal may be especially sensitive to such unnecessary hostility to a witness. Adopt a gentle inquiring approach; it may also cause the witness to ease up and relax and be more willing to agree with your version of events; do not unwittingly adopt Cicero's maxim that 'when you have no basis for argument, abuse the plaintiff'. You do not want the employment tribunal's sympathies to be more with the hunted witness than with the hunting advocate.

(n) Ensure that you put the whole case to each witness: again the tribunal will probably give you time to look over your notes, or even (after a long and difficult cross-examination) may rise for a few minutes for you to be sure that you have covered every point.

(o) Don't allow the other side's witness to state his case better in cross-examination than he did before in examination in chief and do not allow him to introduce in cross-examination whole areas of evidence about which his own advocate has forgotten to ask him.

(p) Don't expect a witness (and this applies to your own side, too) to help you; don't go off on a fishing trip; it is often said that if you try to cast about seeing what turns up, you mostly get old boots and bicycle tyres.

(q) Ensure that each question has a specific purpose.

(r) When you have asked a question, let the witness respond in his own way.

(s) Don't ask questions of the wrong witness.

(t) Don't ask questions apologetically, or tentatively. You should seek to take control of proceedings (subject of course to the overriding authority of the tribunal itself).

(u) Remember in most cases that you are seeking to discredit the evidence of the witness not the witness himself.

(v) Don't ask one question too many – it can be fatal.

6.2.5 Re-examination

You can only re-examine about matters which arose in cross-examination. Remember that by this stage, your witness may be tired, truculent and just want to get home and the tribunal may be bored. Avoid re-examination if you can, that is if the witness has stood up to the rigours of cross-examination unscathed (or virtually so). You also do not want to give the impression to the tribunal that you do not like what a witness said in examination or in cross-examination and want to pick-up the pieces. This approach serves to draw further attention to your weak points. On the other hand, re-examination has been described as 'a much neglected but sinister art form'. In any case, be short and sharp in re-examination and do not traverse old ground again.

6.2.6 Closing speech

Most employment tribunals are impatient with long closing speeches, save in highly complex cases. Your aim should be to bring the various strands of fact and law in the case together in such a way that in effect you write the tribunal's decision for them (or the decision which you wish to see promulgated).

Ensure that the quotations to which you refer from the evidence are 100% accurate. In complex cases, it may be appropriate to use written observations or a skeleton argument. You will probably wish to elaborate them orally, and in many cases, important ideas may arise from interchanges between you and the tribunal members. In any event, go through the evidence in a logical order. Other points to remember:

(a) you must deploy all your legal arguments at this stage, because the EAT will rarely entertain points of law which were not raised in the employment tribunal;

(b) pick a logical structure for the closing speech organised preferably through a series of crisp submissions;

(c) only cite cases if it is necessary to do so. Most employment tribunal chairmen are very familiar with the leading cases and nothing will be gained by a detailed recitation of the facts, for example, of *Devis v Atkin* (1976) ICR 196. Set out simply and clearly the propositions for which you contend; only if the tribunal look puzzled or disapprove of the proposition for which you contend do you need to read the case. Do not cite other employment tribunal decisions to them since they have no authority in other cases;

(d) refer back to the comments made by the chairman and lay members during the hearing, both those which are supportive and those hostile to your case.

6.2.7 Hints

The 'do nots':

(a) Do not engage in theatricalties.

(b) Do not keep interrupting your opponent; if you must object (for example, to a blatantly leading question), do it gracefully, appreciating the difficulties of your opponent.

(c) Do not lounge about, slouch, yawn.

(d) Do not be thrown by a chairman who makes it very clear that he wants the parties to settle the case or that you are going to lose (you may persuade him to change his mind).

The 'do's':

(a) Maintain credibility with the tribunal.

(b) Be brief.

(c) Keep a very careful note of the evidence.

(d) Listen to all the evidence with visible interest.

(e) Even if you are not formally bound by them, have in mind the Bar Rules of Conduct that you 'should guard against being used as a channel for questions which are only intended to insult or annoy either the witness or any other person'.

6.2.8 Miscellaneous points on the hearing

Normally, witnesses take the oath, but they can affirm if they so choose. They are subject to the rules of perjury in the normal way. In England and Wales (but not Scotland) witnesses are permitted to remain in the tribunal room, whilst evidence from other witnesses is heard. Some employment tribunal chairman adopt an inquisitorial role and will themselves question witnesses more directly than may be thought proper for a High Court judge. The clerk will number each set of documents handed in consecutively (A1 for the first of the Applicant's set of documents, A2 for the second, and so on). Seek to agree a bundle.

(a) Do not submit that there is no case to answer after hearing the respondent's evidence; only in an extreme case will an employment tribunal find in favour of an applicant without hearing him give evidence.

(b) Do not use hearsay evidence if it is possible to avoid doing so.

(c) The employment tribunal is directed by its Rules to conduct the hearing in an informal manner. Generally, it is the complete master of its procedure and each chairman approaches the hearing in a different manner. Some are sticklers, for example, for the rule against hearsay; others are more lax.

(d) Tribunals must follow the general principles of natural justice and a fair trial, and should not indicate that they have made up their mind before hearing all the evidence.

(e) The tribunal may allow an unrepresented applicant or respondent to read his statement from the witness table.

(f) You may wish to exchange witness statements, but this is not compulsory in the absence of an order from the tribunal (see *Eurobell Holdings plc v Barker* [1998] ICR 299).

6.3   The decision

The form of the decision

The tribunal may give its decision at the end of the hearing (in which case the chairman will usually dictate it there and then into a recording machine), or it may be reserved. In either case, a written decision will be sent to the parties in due course. Most decisions contain a review of the evidence and the submissions made by the representatives, but to be valid under the rules the decision need only 'tell the parties in broad terms why they lose or, as the case may be, win' according to the Court of Appeal. Where there is a clear conflict of evidence on a central issue of fact, the tribunal should reach a view of that evidence and should not rest on the fact that the burden of proof has not been satisfied.

Summary decisions

Employment tribunals may give their reasons in summary form in dismissal applications save in discrimination cases or interim relief applications. The employment tribunal must also give a decision in extended form if a party asks for one within 21 days of the hearing, and the tribunal has a discretion to do so in any case in which, after summary reasons have been given, it considers that a fuller decision is desirable (Employment Tribunal Rules 1993, r 10).

Public register

The document containing the reasons must be entered in the register of decisions which is open to public inspection unless a specific order is made in a case of sexual misconduct.

Miscellaneous points on decisions

(a) Where the tribunal has reached a majority decision (which is rare), the chairman should clearly set out the opinions of majority and minority in the decision.

(b) The employment tribunal has power of its own motion to correct any simple mistake of fact or calculation which arises from an accidental slip or omission.

6.4 Costs

Costs are only rarely awarded but the employment tribunal:

(a) may make an award where a party has behaved frivolously, vexatiously, abusively, disruptively or otherwise unreasonably in bringing or conducting the proceedings;

(b) must make an award where:

- the proceedings arise out of the respondent's failure to permit the applicant to return to work after an absence due to pregnancy or confinement, and the postponement or adjournment has been caused by the respondent's failure, without a specific reason, to adduce reasonable evidence as the the availability of the job from which the applicant was dismissed, or, as the case may be, which she held before her absence, or of comparable or suitable employment. Where the applicant has expressed a wish to be reinstated or re-engaged which has been communicated to the respondent at least seven days before the hearing (Employment Tribunal Rules 1993, r 12(5)(a)); or

- the proceedings arise out of the respondent's failure to permit the applicant to return to work after an absence due to pregnancy or confinement (Employment Tribunal Rules 1993, r 12(5)(b)).

(c) Employment tribunals have exercised their discretion to award costs where:

- the employer made allegations of criminal conduct against the employee but failed to attend the hearing to substantiate them;

- the employer's representative only gave the employee's representative a large number of documents on the morning of the hearing;

- the application was withdrawn on the date of the hearing;

- the application was brought merely as a bargaining counter in relation to a claim for personal injuries.

It is possible to write a Calderbank letter to the other party, that is, a letter making an offer of settlement which will only be shown to the tribunal at the stage when costs fall to be considered, but it is for the tribunal to decide in each case whether the refusal to accept that offer amounted to unreasonable conduct.

The level of costs

The employment tribunal itself may assess a sum of costs and expenses only up to £500 or (more rarely) it may order that the costs be taxed on the appropriate county court scale by the taxing officer of the county court. The amounts actually awarded are low, and rarely cover the amount expended in legal fees (Employment Tribunal Rules, 1993, r 12(3)(a)). The £500 is likely to be soon increased to £10,000.

The application for costs

The application should be made at the hearing itself or within a reasonable time after the hearing. It may be necessary to await a reserved decision before applying.

Witnesses' expenses

Costs are separate from witness expenses. The parties and their witnesses are entitled to reimbursement for travelling and subsistence expenses, and wages lost through absence from work in attending the employment tribunal. These expenses are paid by the employment tribunal itself. Legal representatives do not qualify for the payment of expenses!

6.5   Review

An employment tribunal may review its decision and confirm, revoke or vary any decision made where:

(a) the decision was wrongly made as a result of an error on the part of the tribunal staff; or

(b) a party did not receive notice of the proceedings leading to the decision; or

(c) the decision was made in the absence of a party or person entitled to be heard; or

(d) new evidence has become available since the conclusion of the hearing to which the decision relates provided that its existence could not have been reasonably known of at the time of the hearing or foreseen; or

(e) the interests of justice require such a review.

6.5.1   Application

An application for review may be made either at the end of the tribunal hearing or more frequently within 14 days of the decision being sent to the parties. The employment tribunal can (but rarely does) review a decision of its own motion. In the latter case, the application is addressed to the Secretary of Employment Tribunals at the relevant ROET. The application should set out the grounds on which it is to be contended that the decision was wrong. The employment tribunal chairman might himself refuse the application for review.

Points to notice

(a) A person seeking a review on the grounds of his absence must give a good excuse for his failure to attend the hearing to justify a review.

(b) Where the ground is new evidence, the party seeking to adduce it must show that the evidence could not have been obtained with due diligence at the time of the hearing.

(c) A review may be heard even though an appeal is being made to the EAT but, in the case of an error of law, the appeal is the more appropriate mechanism.

(d) The application for the review should set out not only the grounds on which the review is sought but also the reasons why it is suggested that the decision reached is incorrect.

6.6 Enforcement of the award

(a) The employment tribunal has no power of enforcement of its own and cannot commit anyone for breach of its orders.

(b) An order for the payment of money may be registered in the appropriate county court.

(c) Where an order for reinstatement or re-engagement is made but disobeyed, the only sanction is an 'additional award' (ERA, s 117) which itself could be enforced like any other award in the county court.

6.6.1 Procedure

The applicant for enforcement applies without notice to the other side to the county court for the district in which the party in default resides or carries on business on a simple form:

(a) verifying the amount remaining due from the defaulting party; and

(b) filing a copy of the relevant award, order or agreement pursuant to which it is claimed that the money is due.

The matter then goes before the county court registrar with an appeal to the county court judge. Execution takes its normal course as if it were a county court judgment.

7 Employment Appeal Tribunal

7.1 EAT

The Employment Appeal Tribunal (EAT) consists in any particular case of a High Court or county judge or a recorder (in England and Wales) or a Court of Session judge (in Scotland) sitting with lay representatives of management and unions. As in the employment tribunal with the consent of the parties, the judge and one lay member may sit to hear a case. Further, a judge may sit alone to hear any appeal from a chairman sitting alone.

7.1.1 Venue

The EAT normally sits at Audit House, 58 Victoria Embankment, London and 52 Melville Street, Edinburgh. It may, however, sit anywhere it wishes in Great Britain, and now sits in Cardiff from time to time.

7.1.2 Rules

The procedure before the EAT is regulated by Pt II of the Employment Tribunals Act 1996 and the Employment Appeal Tribunal Rules 1993. The EAT Practice Direction, dated 29 March 1996, regulates matters of detail.

7.2   Scope of appeal

7.2.1 Point of law

To succeed in an appeal, the employment tribunal must have wrongly applied a legal principle, misunderstood a statute or reached a decision which is perverse in the sense that no reasonable employment tribunal properly directed could have reached such a decision, so that the EAT says 'My goodness, that was certainly wrong', as May LJ put it (commonly dubbed 'the Biggles test'). An appeal will not succeed merely because the EAT would have reached a different decision. (See *BT plc v Sheridan* [1990] IRLR 27).

An appeal will fail if:

(a) it is based on the fact that an employment tribunal has not expressly mentioned a factor in its decision;

(b) the contention is that one employment tribunal has reached one conclusion and another has reached a different conclusion on similar facts;

(c) a point is raised for the first time before the EAT.

The following have been held to be essentially questions of fact for the employment tribunal to decide:

(a) whether an employee has been constructively dismissed;

(b) whether an employee is guilty of contributory fault;

(c) whether a person has engaged in industrial action;

(d) whether an employee has been unfairly dismissed;

(e) when and whether a transfer of an undertaking took place; and

(f) the level of awards for injury to feelings in discrimination cases.

7.2.2 Remission

The EAT may overturn a decision by the employment tribunal or remit a case to the employment tribunal if it sees fit, and where there has been a misdirection in law by the employment tribunal, the EAT should remit the case for rehearing by the same or a different employment tribunal unless the decision is 'plainly and unarguably right notwithstanding that misdirection': *Dobie v Burns International Security Services Ltd* [1984] ICR 812.

7.2.3 Cases the EAT will not hear

The EAT is likely to refuse to hear an appeal where:

(a) the point under appeal is now wholly academic because the result of the appeal would have no practical consequence on the parties; or

(b) the point was not raised before the employment tribunal and it would require further evidence to be called to deal with the issue unless the matter goes to the jurisdiction of the employment tribunal as, for example, in *Jones v Governing Body of Burdett Coutts School* [1999] ICR 38.

7.2.4 Instituting an appeal

An appeal to the EAT must be instituted by serving a notice of appeal on the EAT within 42 days of 'the date on which reasons in extended form for the decision or order of the employment tribunal were sent to the parties'. An appeal may be made on the issue of liability even though compensation or any other remedy has yet to be determined. The EAT may, however, permit or authorise the institution of an appeal notwithstanding that the extended written reasons have not yet been given. Legal aid is available for appealing or defending an appeal in the EAT. The registrar of the EAT is responsible for serving the notice of appeal and Respondent's Answer on the other party.

An application for extension of the time for appealing may be made. It is not in itself a sufficient reason that the appellant was applying for legal aid or seeking support from the Commission for Racial Equality, Equal Opportunities Commission, Disability Rights Commission or a trade union. These time limits are usually strictly adhered to by the EAT.

The EAT Registrar may inform the appellant that his grounds of appeal do not appear to the registrar to give to the EAT jurisdiction, and that no further action will be taken on the appeal unless the President or a judge of the EAT so directs. The appellant may serve a fresh notice of appeal within the time remaining for presenting an appeal, or within 28 days from the date when he was sent the Registrar's notification, whichever period be the longer (EAT Rules, r 3(3)).

7.2.5 Preliminary hearing

All appeals are now listed for a preliminary and directions hearing before the full EAT. It is for the appellant then to show that he has a fairly arguable point of law fit to go to a full hearing. Such preliminary hearings are usually listed for no more than 45 minutes.

7.2.6 Grounds of appeal

The appellant should be as specific as possible in his grounds of appeal and should not make generalised allegations, such as 'the decision was contrary to the evidence'.

7.2.7 Action by respondent

The respondent may rely before the EAT on the reason given in the decision of the employment tribunal or seek to put forward other grounds to support the decision. He may file a cross-appeal if he wishes to challenge the decision or order in any way. He is sent a standard form for the Respondent's Answer by the EAT in any event.

7.2.8 New evidence

The EAT will only receive evidence which was not before the employment tribunal where the evidence could not have been obtained with due diligence at the time of the tribunal hearing. It would normally be appropriate in such a case to present an affidavit to the EAT with the outline of the evidence which it is sought to adduce. The EAT will consider this without necessarily deciding when it should be admitted.

7.2.9 Bundle of documents

The EAT office itself prepares copies of all documents for the use of the judge and members at the EAT hearing and a copy of the index of these documents is sent to the parties some time prior to the hearing. If the parties consider that other documents are necessary for the EAT's consideration of the case, they should contact the EAT in good time before the hearing of the appeal and provide copies of the documents. (See Bowers, J, Brown, D and Mead, G, Employment Tribunal Practice and Procedure, 3rd edn, 1999.)

7.3 The hearing

7.3.1 Notes of evidence

The EAT hears no evidence but may have available to it the notes of evidence. The employment tribunal Chairman has a duty to take a note of all the evidence presented to the tribunal at the hearing. The notes will be sent to the parties only if the EAT is 'satisfied that all or parts of such notes are *necessary* for the purpose of arguing the point of law on the appeal' (EAT Practice Direction, 29 March 1996). The EAT is unwilling to allow parties to use the notes as a 'fishing expedition', if they do not have proper grounds for appeal without them.

The EAT will only rarely look at the notes taken by a party or his representatives before the employment tribunal. When a party claims that the chairman's notes are inaccurate, the EAT requires an affidavit or witness statement to support such an allegation.

7.3.2 Interlocutory issues

The EAT Registrar determines any interlocutory application to the EAT in the best way justly and economically to dispose of the case (EAT Rules, rr 19–22). He/she may, thus, hear applications to amend the notice of appeal, consolidate cases and introduce new evidence. Where a decision is made against a party's interest, the party may appeal to the judge within three days of the registrar's decision being made.

The EAT has power under its rules to debar a party to an appeal who has not complied with any of its orders (EAT Rules, r 26); to order documents to be produced or witnesses to attend in the rare event that new evidence is received (r 27); to join other parties (r 18).

7.3.3 Listing

A list is prepared by the EAT each month of the cases to be heard on specific dates in that month. Parties must give an estimate of the likely duration of the appeal and keep the EAT informed if that estimate alters for any reason.

7.3.4 Costs

The EAT can award costs in the same circumstances as the employment tribunal. The EAT is likely to make such an award when an appeal is abandoned shortly before or at the hearing, or where there is no arguable point of law. Where costs are awarded, the EAT may assess the appropriate sum at once or send the matter for taxation (EAT Rules, r 34).

8 Sources and Institutions

8.1 ACAS

The Advisory Conciliation and Arbitration Service (ACAS) was established by the Employment Protection Act 1975 and took over the duties of the Commission on Industrial Relations. The ACAS Council consists of a chairman and part time members drawn from both sides of industry. ACAS provides conciliation services in industrial disputes; arranges for arbitration if required; formulates Codes of Practice for submission to the Secretary of State for Trade and Industry, and employs Conciliation Officers to deal with individual complaints to employment tribunals (see 5.3). 'It is the general duty of ACAS to promote the improvement of industrial relations.' (s 26 of the Employment Relations Act 1999).

8.2 CAC

The Central Arbitration Committee decides on applications for trade unions recognition, hears complaints about non-disclosure of information which impedes collective bargaining (s 183 of the Trade Union and Labour Relations (Consolidation) Act 1992 (TULR(C)A)) and provides voluntary arbitration facilities when cases are referred by ACAS.

8.3 Certification Officer

The main roles of the Certification Officer are to:

(a) keep a list of trade unions and employers' associations;

(b) deal with political expenditure by trade unions under the TULR(C)A 1992;

(c) supervise amalgamations of trade unions under the TULR(C)A 1992;

(d) hear applications for breach of the requirement that unions elect their executive committees by secret ballot (TULR(C)A 1992).

There is an appeal on matters of fact and law to the Employment Appeal Tribunal.

9 Forms

9.1   IT1: application to an employment tribunal

Application to an Employment Tribunal

For office use

Received at ET

- If you fax this form you do not need to send one in the post.
- This form has to be photocopied. Please use CAPITALS and black ink (if possible).
- Where there are tick boxes, please tick the one that applies.

Case number

Code

Initials

1 Please give the type of complaint you want the tribunal to decide (for example, unfair dismissal, equal pay). A full list is available from the tribunal office. If you have more than one complaint list them all.

2 Please give your details

Mr ☐ Mrs ☐ Miss ☐ Ms ☐ Other _____

First names

Surname

Date of birth

Address

Postcode

Phone number

Daytime phone number

Please give an address to which we should send documents if different from above

Postcode

3 If a representative is acting for you please give details
(all correspondence will be sent to your representative)

Name

Address

Postcode

Phone

Fax

Reference

4 Please give the dates of your employment

From _____ to _____

5 Please give the name and address of the employer, other organisation or person against whom this complaint is being brought

Name

Address

Postcode

Phone number

Please give the place where you worked or applied to work if different from above

Address

Postcode

6 Please say what job you did for the employer (or what job you applied for). If this does not apply, please say what your connection was with the employer

IT1(E/W)

7 Please give the number of normal basic hours worked each week

Hours per week

8 Please give your earning details

Basic wage or salary

£   :   per

Average take home pay

£   :   per

Other bonuses or benefits

£   :   per

9 If your complaint is not about dismissal, please give the date when the matter you are complaining about took place

10 Unfair dismissal applicants only

Please indicate what you are seeking at this stage, if you win your case

☐ Reinstatement: to carry on working in your old job as before (an order for reinstatement normally includes an award of compensation for loss of earnings).

☐ Re-engagement: to start another job or new contract with your old employer (an order for re-engagement normally includes an award of compensation for loss of earnings).

☐ Compensation only: to get an award of money

11 Please give details of your complaint

If there is not enough space for your answer, please continue on a separate sheet and attach it to this form.

12 Please sign and date this form, then send it to the appropriate address on the back cover of this booklet, (see postcode list on pages 13-16).

Signed

Date

IT1(E/W)

9.2   IT3: notice of appearance by respondent

EMPLOYMENT TRIBUNALS

Telephone
Fax

In the application of

Case Number
(please quote in all correspondence)

* This form has to be photocopied, if possible please use Black Ink and Capital letters
* If there is not enough space for your answer, please continue on a separate sheet and attach it to this form

1. Full name and address of the Respondent:	3. Do you intend to resist the application? (Tick appropriate box)
	YES NO
	4. Was the applicant dismissed? (Tick appropriate box)
	YES NO
	Please give reason below
	Reason for dismissal:
	5. Are the dates of employment given by the applicant correct? (Tick appropriate box)
Post Code:	YES NO
Telephone number:	please give correct dates below
2. If you require documents and notices to be sent to a representative or any other address in the United Kingdom please give details:	Began on
	Ended on
	6. Are the details given by the applicant about wages/salary, take home or other bonuses correct? (Tick appropriate box)
	YES NO
	Please give correct details below
	Basic Wages/Salary £ per
	Average Take Home Pay £ per
	Other Bonuses/Benefits £ per
	PLEASE TURN OVER
	for office use only
	Date of receipt Initials
Post Code:	
Reference:	
Telephone number:	

Form IT3 E&W - 8/98

7. Give particulars of the grounds on which you intend to resist the application.

8. Please sign and date the form.

Signed   Dated

DATA PROTECTION ACT 1984
We may put some of the information you give on this form on to a computer. This helps us to monitor progress and produce statistics. We may also give information to:
* the other party in the case
* other parts of the DTI and organisations such as ACAS (Advisory Conciliation and Arbitration Service), the Equal Opportunities Commission or the Commission for Racial Equality.

Please post or fax this form to :

* IF YOU FAX THE FORM, DO NOT POST A COPY AS WELL
* IF YOU POST THE FORM, TAKE A COPY FOR YOUR RECORDS

Form IT3 E&W - 8/98

9.3 Notice of appeal from decision of employment tribunal

1   The appellant is [*name and address of appellant*].

2   Any communication relating to this appeal may be sent to the appellant at [*appellant's address for service, including telephone number, if any*].

3   The appellant appeals from [*here give particulars of the decision of the employment tribunal from which the appeal is brought including the date*].

4   The parties to the proceedings before the employment tribunal, other than the appellant, were [*names and addresses of other parties to the proceedings resulting in decision appealed from*].

5   A copy of the employment tribunal's decision or order and of the extended written reasons for that decision or order are attached to this notice.

6   The grounds upon which this appeal is brought are that the employment tribunal erred in law in that [*here set out in paragraphs the various grounds of appeal*].

Date: _____ Signed: _____

9.4 Appeal from decision of employment tribunal/certification officer: respondent's answer

1 The respondent is [*name and address of respondent*]:–

2 Any communication relating to this appeal may be sent to the respondent at [*respondent's address for service, including telephone number, if any*]:–

3 The respondent intends to resist the appeal of [*here give name of appellant*]:

The grounds on which the respondent will rely are [the grounds relied upon by the employment tribunal/Certification Officer for making the decision or order appealed from] [and] [the following grounds]:–

[*here set out grounds which differ from those relied upon by the employment tribunal or Certification Officer, as case may be*]:

4 The respondent cross-appeals from
[*here give particulars of the decision appealed from*]:–

5 The respondent's grounds of appeal are
[*here state the grounds of appeal*]:–

Date: _____ Signed: _____

For other forms, see *Atkin's Court Forms,* Vol 38, 1999.

10 Time Limits

As set out in Bowers, J, Brown, D and Mead, G, *Employment Tribunal Practice and Procedure,* 3rd edn, 1999, Vol 2, pp 81–94.

Employment right and statutory provision	When application must be made
1 Unfair dismissal: Employment Rights Act 1996 (ERA), s 98 and s 111(2)	1 (i) Before effective date of termination if employee is dismissed with notice: ERA 1996, s 111(4); or (ii) within three months from effective date of termination; but (iii) in the case of unfair selection of strikers for re-engagement, six months from applicant's date of dismissal: TULR(C)A 1992, s 239(2).
2 Consultation over redundancy: TULR(C)A 1992, s 188	2 Before the proposed dismissal or three months from the date on which the dismissal takes effect: TULR(C)A 1992, s 189(5).
3 Protective award claim by trade union for failing to consult over redundancies: TULR(C)A 1992, s 192	3 Three months from the date when the application of failure to pay was made: TULR(C)A 1992, s 192(2).
4 Race discrimination in employment: Race Relations Act 1976, s 54	4 Three months from the date when the act complained of was done: Race Relations Act 1976, s 68(1) and (6).

Action an applicant must take within the time limit	Discretionary power to extend time limit
1 Present application to an employment tribunal	1 Such further period as the employment tribunal considers reasonable in a case where it is satisfied it was not reasonably practicable for the application to be presented before the end of the period of three months.
2 Present a complaint	2 As in unfair dismissal
3 Present application to an employment tribunal	3 As in unfair dismissal
4 Present application to an employment tribunal	4 Just and equitable: ERA 1996, s 68(6)

Employment right and statutory provision	When application must be made
5 Reasons for dismissal: ERA 1996, s 93	5 Three months from the effective date of termination: ERA 1996, s 93(3)
6 Redundancy payment: ERA 1996, s 166	6 Within six months of the relevant date of termination: ERA 1996, s 164
7 Sex discrimination in employment: Sex Discrimination Act 1975, s 63	7 Three months from the date when the act complained of was done: SDA 1975, s 176(1)
8 Time off to look for work or training on redundancy: ERA 1996, s 52	8 Three months from the date of refusal of time off: ERA 1996, s 54(2)

Action an applicant must take within the time limit	Discretionary power to extend time limit
5 Present application to an employment tribunal	5 As in unfair dismissal
6 (i) Refer a question as to the right of the employee to the payment or as to the amount of the payment to an employment tribunal; or (ii) present a complaint of unfair dismissal to an employment tribunal with redundancy as the reason for dismissal	6 Just and equitable: ERA 1996, s 164(2)
7 Present application to an employment tribunal	7 Just and equitable
8 Present application to an employment tribunal	8 As in unfair dismissal

11 Further Reading

Employment law

Barrow, C, *Industrial Relations Law*, 1999, London: Cavendish Publishing

Bowers, J, *Bowers on Employment Law*, 5th edn, 2000, London: Blackstone

Bowers, J and Honeyball, S, *Textbook on Employment Law*, 6th edn, 2000, London: Blackstone

Crump, DW and Pugsley, D, *Contracts of Employment*, 7th edn, 1997, London: Butterworths

Davies, P and Freedland, M, *Labour Law, Text and Materials*, 2nd edn, 1984, London: Weidenfeld & Nicholson

Deakin, S and Morris, G, *Labour Law*, 1998, London: Sweet & Maxwell

Lamb, N, *Remedies in the Employment Tribunal*, 1998, London: Sweet & Maxwell

Osman, C *et al*, *Employment Law Guide*, 2nd edn, 1996, London: Butterworths

Rideout, R *et al*, *Principles of Labour Law*, 4th edn, 1983, London: Sweet & Maxwell

Selwyn, N, *Law of Employment*, 7th edn, 1991, London: Butterworths

Slade, E, *Tolley's Employment Handbook*, 9th edn, 2000, Croydon: Tolley

Smith, IT and Wood, JC, *Industrial Law*, 6th edn, 1996, London: Butterworths

Wallington, P, *Butterworths' Employment Law Handbook,* 9th edn, 2000, London: Butterworths (collection of statutes)

Wedderburn (Lord), *The Worker and the Law*, 3rd edn, 1987, Harmondsworth: Penguin

Looseleaf works

Harvey, R, *Harvey on Industrial Relations and Employment Law*, 6 Vols, 2001, London: Butterworths

Hepple, RA and O'Higgins, D, *Hepple and O'Higgins' Encyclopedia on Industrial Relations and Employment Law*, 2001, London: Sweet & Maxwell

Employment tribunal procedure

Bowers, J, 'Trade Labour and Employment', *Atkins Court Forms,* Vol 38, 1999, London: Butterworths

Bowers, J, Brown, D and Mead, G, *Employment Tribunal Practice and Procedure*, 3rd edn, 1999, London: Sweet & Maxwell

Unfair dismissal

Anderman, S, *The Law of Unfair Dismissal*, 2nd edn, 1995, London: Butterworths

Barnett, D, *Avoiding Unfair Dismissals*, 1999, Chichester: Wiley

Korn, A, *Compensation for Dismissal*, 2nd edn, 1999, London: Blackstone

Mead, G, *Unfair Dismissal*, 5th edn, 1994, London: Longman

Upex, R, *The Law of Termination of Employment*, 1997, London: Sweet & Maxwell

Duggan, M, *Unfair Dismissal, Law Practice and Evidence,* 2000, London: CLT

Special issues

Bourne, C and Whitmore, J, *Anti-Discrimination Law in Britain*, 3rd edn, 1996, London: Sweet & Maxwell

Doyle, B, *Disability and Discrimination, the New Law*, 1996, Bristol: Jordans

Palmer, C, *Maternity Rights*, 2nd edn, 2000, London: LAG

Pollard, D, *Corporate Insolvency: Employment and Pensions Rights*, 2nd edn, 2000, London: Butterworths

Randall, N and Smith, I, *A Guide to the Employment Relations Act 1999*, 1999, London: Butterworths

Bowers, J and Duggan, M, *The Modern Law of Strikes*, 1987, London: FTP

Brearley, K and Bloch, S, *Employment Covenants and Confidential Information – Law, Practice and Technique*, 2nd edn, 1999, London: Butterworths

Elias, P and Bowers, J, *Transfers of Undertakings: The Legal Pitfalls*, Professional Intelligence Report, 6th edn, 1996, London: Longman

Fagan, N, *Contracts of Employment*, 1990, London: Sweet & Maxwell

Fredman, S and Morris, G, *The State as Employer*, 1990, London: Mansell

Honeyball, S, *Sex, Employment and the Law*, 1991, Oxford: Blackwell

Julyon, A, *Service Agreements*, 5th edn, 1986, London: Longman

McMullen, J, *Business Transfers and Employee Rights*, 2000, London: Butterworths (looseleaf with regular updating)

Mehigan, S and Griffiths, D, *Restraint of Trade and Business Secrets*, 3rd edn, 1996, London: FT Law & Tax

Evidence and advocacy

Foster, C *et al*, *Civil Advocacy: A Practical Guide*, 2nd edn, 2001 (forthcoming), London: Cavendish Publishing

Bowers, J and Gatt, I, *Procedure in Courts and Tribunals*, 2nd edn, 2000, London: Cavendish Publishing

Evans, K, *Advocacy at the Bar*, 1983, London: Financial Training

Journals

Incomes Data Service Brief produces useful handbooks (bi-monthly)

Industrial Relations Legal Information Bulletin, Industrial Relations Services (bi-monthly)

Industrial Law Journal, OUP (quarterly)

Employment Lawyer, CCH (bi-monthly)

Codes of practice

ACAS 1: *Disciplinary Practice and Procedures in Employment* (1977)

ACAS 2: *Disclosure of Information to Trade Unions for Collective Bargaining Purposes* (1977)

ACAS 3: *Time off for Trade Union Duties and Activities* (1991)

Health and Safety Commission: *Safety Representatives and Safety Committees* (1978)

Health and Safety Commission: *Time off for the Training of Safety Representatives* (1978)

Department of Employment Code of Practice: *Picketing* (1992)

Department of Employment Code of Practice: *Trade Union Ballots on Industrial Action* (1991)

Commission for Racial Equality: *Code of Practice for the Elimination of Racial Discrimination and the Promotion of Equality of Opportunity in Employment* (1983)

Equal Opportunities Commission: *Code of Practice for the Elimination of Discrimination on the Grounds of Sex and Marriage and the Promotion of Equality of Opportunity in Employment* (1985)

12 Useful Addresses

Employment Tribunals

Central Office of the Employment Tribunals (England and Wales)

100 Southgate Street
Bury St Edmunds
Suffolk IP33 2AQ
Tel: 01284 762 300
Fax: 01284 766 334

Regional Offices of the Employment Tribunals (England and Wales)

Birmingham

Phoenix House
1–3 Newhall Street
Birmingham B3 3NH
Tel: 0121 236 6051
Fax: 0121 236 6029

Bristol

Regional Office
Ground Floor
The Crescent Centre
Temple Beck
Bristol BS1 6EZ
Tel: 0117 929 8261
Fax: 0117 925 3452

Office of the Employment Tribunals
Renslade House
Bonhay Road
Exeter EX4 3BX
Tel: 01392 279665
Fax: 01392 430063

Bury St Edmunds

Regional Office
100 Southgate Street
Bury St Edmunds
Suffolk IP33 2AQ
Tel: 01284 762 171
Fax: 01284 766 334

Office of the Employment Tribunals
8–10 Howard Street
Bedford MK40 3HS
Tel: 01234 351306
Fax: 01234 352315

Cardiff

Regional Office
Caradog House
1–6 St Andrew's Place
Cardiff CF1 3BE
Tel: 029 2037 2693
Fax: 029 2022 5906

Office of the Employment Tribunals
Prospect House
Belle Vue Road
Shrewsbury SY3 7AR
Tel: 01743 358 341
Fax: 01743 244 186

Leeds

Regional Office
3rd Floor
11 Albion Street
Leeds LS1 5ES
Tel: 0113 245 9741
Fax: 0113 242 8843

Office of Employment Tribunals
14 East Parade
Sheffield S1 2ET
Tel: 0114 276 0348
Fax: 0114 276 2551

London (Central)

19–29 Woburn Place
London WC1H 0LU
Tel: 020 7273 8525
Fax: 020 7273 8686

London (East)

44 The Broadway
London E15

London (South)

Regional Office
Montague Court
101 London Road
Croydon CR0 2RF
Tel: 020 8667 9131
Fax: 020 8649 9470

Office of the Employment Tribunals
Tufton House
Tufton Street
Ashford
Kent TN23 1RJ
Tel: 01233 621 346
Fax: 01233 624 423

Manchester

Regional Office
Alexandra House
14–22 The Parsonage
Manchester M3 2JA
Tel: 0161 833 0581
Fax: 0161 832 0249

Office of Employment Tribunals
1st Floor, Cunard Building,
Pier Head
Liverpool L3 1TS
Tel: 0151 236 9397
Fax: 0151 231 1484

Newcastle-upon-Tyne

Quayside House
110 Quayside
Newcastle-upon-Tyne NE1 6NF
Tel: 0191 2606900
Fax: 0191 222 1680

Nottingham

Regional Office
3rd Floor
Byron House
2A Maid Marion Way
Nottingham NG1 6HS
Tel: 0115 947 5701
Fax: 0115 950 7612

Office of the Employment Tribunals
5A New Walk
Leicester LE1 6TE
Tel: 0116 255 0099
Fax: 0116 255 6099

Reading

30–31 Friar Street
Reading RG1 1DY
Tel: 0118 9594 917/9
Fax: 0118 9568 066

Southampton

Regional Office
3rd Floor
Duke's Keep
Marsh Lane
Southampton SO1 1EX
Tel: 023 8063 9555

Fax: 023 8063 5506
Office of the Employment Tribunals
St James House
New England Street
Brighton BN1 4GQ
Tel: 01273 571 488
Fax: 01273 623 645

Central Office of the Employment Tribunals (Scotland)

215 Bothwell Street
Glasgow G2 7TS
Tel: 0141 204 0730
Fax: 0141 204 0732

Regional offices of the Employment Tribunals (Scotland)

Aberdeen Office
84–88 Guild Street
Aberdeen AB1 6LT
Tel: 01224 593 137
Fax: 01224 593 138

Dundee Office
13 Albert Square
Dundee DD1 1DD
Tel: 01382 221 578
Fax: 01382 227 136

Employment Appeal Tribunal

Central Office
Audit House
58 Victoria Embankment
London EC4Y 0DS
Tel: 020 7273 1041
Fax: 020 7273 1045

Other useful addresses

Equal Opportunities Commission
Arndale House
Arndale Centre
Manchester M3 3EQ
Tel: 0161 838 8312
Fax: 0161 835 1657

Edinburgh Office
124–125 Princes Street
Edinburgh EH2 4AD
0131 2265584

Glasgow Office
St Andrews House
141 West Nile Street
Glasgow G1 2RU
Tel: 0141 3311601
Fax: 0141 3323316

Commission for Racial Equality
Elliott House
10–12 Allington Street
London SW1E 5EH
Tel: 020 7828 7022
Fax: 020 7630 7605